Cambridge Elements ≡

Elements in Development Economics
Series Editor-in-Chief
Kunal Sen
UNU-WIDER and University of Manchester

T0302105

VARIETIES OF STRUCTURAL TRANSFORMATION

Patterns, Determinants, and Consequences

Kunal Sen
UNU-WIDER and University of Manchester

UNU
WIDER

CAMBRIDGE
UNIVERSITY PRESS

Shaftesbury Road, Cambridge CB2 8EA, United Kingdom

One Liberty Plaza, 20th Floor, New York, NY 10006, USA

477 Williamstown Road, Port Melbourne, VIC 3207, Australia

314–321, 3rd Floor, Plot 3, Splendor Forum, Jasola District Centre,
New Delhi – 110025, India

103 Penang Road, #05–06/07, Visioncrest Commercial, Singapore 238467

Cambridge University Press is part of Cambridge University Press & Assessment,
a department of the University of Cambridge.

We share the University's mission to contribute to society through the pursuit of
education, learning and research at the highest international levels of excellence.

www.cambridge.org
Information on this title: www.cambridge.org/9781009449915

DOI: 10.1017/9781009449939

First published 2023

A catalogue record for this publication is available from the British Library

ISBN 978-1-009-44991-5 Hardback
ISBN 978-1-009-44995-3 Paperback
ISSN 2755-1601 (online)
ISSN 2755-1598 (print)

Additional resources for this publication at www.cambridge.org/kunalsen

Varieties of Structural Transformation

Patterns, Determinants, and Consequences

Elements in Development Economics

DOI: 10.1017/9781009449939
First published online: August 2023

Kunal Sen
UNU-WIDER and University of Manchester
Author for correspondence: Kunal Sen, sen@wider.unu.edu

Abstract: One of the key features of modern economic growth is the process of structural transformation, which is the movement of workers from agriculture to manufacturing and services. In this study, the author identifies different routes to structural transformation that we see in the developing world. They address the theoretical, empirical, and policy implications of the 'varieties of structural transformation' in low- and middle-income countries. Firstly, using a comparable high-quality data set, they set out the stylized facts of structural transformation across the developing world. Secondly, they assess the classical and neoclassical approaches to structural transformation and review the recent theoretical developments in the literature. Thirdly, they undertake descriptive and econometric analysis of the drivers of structural transformation, and the relationship between structural transformation and inequality. Finally, they assess the policy implications of the study for developing countries. This title is also available as Open Access on Cambridge Core.

Keywords: structural transformation, economic growth, low-income countries, inequality, Economic Transformation Database

ISBNs: 9781009449915 (HB), 9781009449953 (PB), 9781009449939 (OC)
ISSNs: 2755-1601 (online), 2755-1598 (print)

Contents

1 Setting the Stage   1

2 Theories of Structural Transformation   7

3 A Typology of Stages of Structural Transformation   19

4 Patterns of Structural Transformation   27

5 Drivers of Structural Transformation   56

6 The Kuznets Process: Structural Transformation
   and Inequality   78

7 So What Have We Learned?   91

   References   97

   An online appendix for this publication can be accessed
   at www.cambridge.org/kunalsen

1 Setting the Stage

Economists have long searched for patterns that relate successful economic development to structure and policy. This comparative approach in development economics was initiated by Simon Kuznets and predicated on 'the existence of common, transnational factors and a mechanism of interactions among nations that will produce some systematic order in the way modern economic growth can be expected to spread around the world' (Kuznets 1959: 170).[1] One of the most striking findings of this comparative approach to economic development was the universal inverse association of income and the share of agriculture in income and employment. A key feature of modern economic growth was the movement of workers from agriculture to manufacturing and services (Kuznets and Murphy 1966; Chenery and Taylor 1968; Timmer 2013). As noted by Kuznets, in his Nobel Prize lecture delivered in 1971, modern economic growth had six characteristics, and perhaps the most important of these characteristics was structural transformation, which Kuznets defined as 'the shift away from agriculture to non-agricultural pursuits, and recently, away from industry to services; a change in the scale of productive units and a related shift from personal enterprise to impersonal organization of economic firms, with a corresponding change in the occupational status of labour' (Kuznets 1973: 3).

The comparative approach identified the manufacturing sector as the engine of economic growth for most countries and the rate at which industrialization occurred differentiated successful countries from unsuccessful ones (Lewis 1954; Kuznets 1965, 1966; McMillan et al. 2014). The movement of workers from agriculture to manufacturing, and then to services is the path of structural transformation that has been witnessed in all countries which comprise the high-income club as well as the successful growth experiences of East Asia. This path of structural transformation has received a great deal of attention among economists, and underpins most of the theoretical understanding of structural transformation all the way from scholars in classical economics – such as Kuznets, Lewis, Chenery, Syrquin – to more modern approaches that are rooted in the neoclassical tradition (see Herrendorf et al. 2014). Such a view underpins the well-known argument of Kuznets, who argued that structural transformation can lead to higher inequality, at least initially (the so-called 'Kuznets process').

---

[1] In the 1950s, led by economists like Hollis Chenery, Moses Syrquin, and Simon Kuznets, a programme of research (called the 'structural research program' by Chenery 1988) was developed to understand the features and preconditions of modern economic growth (Lewis 1954; Chenery and Syrquin 1975; Syrquin 1988). Core to this research was the interest in understanding 'the interrelated processes of structural change that accompany economic development ... jointly referred to as structural transformation' (Syrquin 1988: 206).

Indeed, the emblematic view of structural transformation as a process of movement of workers first from agriculture to manufacturing, then on to services remains a powerful unifying vision of the process of economic development among both scholars and policymakers.

How likely is the path of structural transformation – the movement of workers from agriculture to manufacturing, and then on to services – that was identified by economists such as Hollis Chenery, Moses Syrquin, and Simon Kuznets as a characteristic of modern economic growth – for low- and middle-income countries today? What are the patterns of structural transformation that we observe in the developing world? What have been the advances in our theoretical understanding of the process of structural transformation? What do we know about the drivers of structural transformation? What are the consequences of structural transformation, especially for inequality? In this Element, we will assess what we know about the patterns, drivers, and consequences of structural transformation using a recently released high-quality data set on sectoral employment and production for fifty-one low-income and middle-income countries from 1990 to 2018. In our analysis of structural transformation, we will follow the comparative approach to economic development pioneered by Chenery, Kuznets, and Syrquin where 'intercountry comparisons play an essential part in understanding the processes of economic and social development' (Chenery and Syrquin 1975: 3). By adopting the comparative approach, we will attempt to identify uniform features of development for groups of countries and examine alternative hypotheses about the causes of structural transformation. A key feature of this approach was to separate 'universal factors' from characteristics that are specific to any particular country (Chenery and Syrquin 1975).

A building block of the comparative approach that we will adopt in this Element is the use of a typology to understand the comparative experience of countries through 'common features and patterns' (Syrquin 1988: 216). We will follow this approach in searching for common features across groups of countries, and not focus on any specific country in the Element.[2] Similar to the earlier comparative approach, we will not analyse the process of structural transformation by region, as using regions as units of analysis (e.g., sub-Saharan Africa versus Asia) does not allow us to see the common features of structural transformation that cuts across regions. The typology we use will classify countries by stages or paths of structural transformation – and our approach is similar to other typological approaches to economic development such as the

---

[2] A different approach, focusing on individual country case-studies, is provided by Alisjahbana et al. (2022).

stages of economic growth proposed by W.W. Rostow (1960) and the agricultural paths of structural transformation by Hayami and Ruttan (1985). More description of our typological approach will be provided in Section 3.

While the period of analysis of the patterns of structural transformation by the classical economists was mostly for the 1950s to the 1970s, there have been several attempts by economists to document patterns of structural transformation for both developed and developing countries from the 1980s to the 2000s using data sets such as the ten-sector data set of the Groningen Growth and Development Centre (GGDC) or that produced by the International Labour Organization (ILO) (see, for example, Dabla-Norris et al. 2013; Herrendorf et al. 2014; Timmer et al. 2015; Nayyar 2019). However, as we will argue in Section 3 of the Element, the analysis of structural transformation in the recent literature is mostly confined to developed and some middle-income countries, and we know very little about the paths of structural transformation followed by low-income countries in Africa and Asia. In addition, past studies have used data sets that do not provide comparable sectoral data for developing countries (such as that provided by ILO), so it is very difficult to assess what we can learn from such intercountry comparisons, with non-comparable data across countries and over time. Furthermore, since the ten-sector GGDC data set (which provides rigorous comparable sectoral data across countries and over time) ends in 2010, we do not know what may have happened to structural transformation since 2010, in a period where many countries in Africa and Asia witnessed rapid economic growth. In this Element, we use the Economic Transformation Database (ETD) produced by the Groningen Growth and UNU-WIDER, which has comparable sectoral data for a range of low- and middle-income countries from 1990 to 2018. We provide more information about ETD in Section 3, discussing its strengths over other similar data sets.

The Role of Manufacturing and Services in Structural Transformation

One of the central tenets in our understanding of economic development is that industrialization lies on the road to economic development (Gollin 2018). As labour and other resources move from agriculture to manufacturing, per capita incomes increase, and economic growth is likely to result.[3] This has been the experience of the advanced market economies and the 'miracle growth'

---

[3] However, structural change – the move of labour from low-productivity to high-productivity sectors – does not necessarily have to be growth enhancing, as documented by McMillan et al. (2014). As they show, structural change in Latin America and Africa in the 1990s has been growth-reducing, though in the case of Africa, after 2000, structural change contributed positively to overall productivity growth.

economies of East Asia (see Krueger 1978, 1980; Riedel 1988). Therefore, industrialization[4] is an important driver of employment growth and poverty reduction in developing countries. At the early stage of transition from an agrarian economy to a modern economy, the manufacturing sector in the typical developing economy has greater potential to absorb surplus labour compared to the services sector, which in the typical low-income country is dominated by informal services. While it is feasible to move unskilled workers from agriculture into better-paid jobs in manufacturing activities, it is not feasible to move them into the formal services sector. Formal services sectors such as banking, insurance, finance, communications, and information technology are characterized by relatively low employment elasticity, and also employment in these sectors requires at least upper secondary school–level education. Unskilled workers can find employment only in informal services such as retail trade and distribution, passenger transport, and construction where wages and productivity are often low. By contrast, employment in manufacturing, particularly in traditional labour-intensive industries such as clothing and footwear, requires mostly on-the-job training (Athukorala and Sen 2014).[5] However, after countries reach a certain level of economic development, the structure of employment and production shifts towards services and away from manufacturing, leading to a hump-shaped nature of manufacturing employment and value-added shares as per capita incomes increase.

An extensive literature has examined the role of industrialization in the structural transformation process (see Chenery 1982 and Syrquin and Chenery 1989 for the earlier literature, and UNIDO 2013, Felipe et al. 2015, and IMF 2018 for the more recent literature). In this short monograph, we do not review the entire literature, but highlight two debates that have come up in the recent literature that is relevant for our purpose. A first area of debate has been on whether today's low- and middle-income countries are following the same path of industrialization in the preliminary stages of economic development as witnessed by the rich countries earlier. Rodrik (2016) documents a significant de-industrialization trend in recent decades that goes beyond the advanced market economies. This phenomenon is particularly noticeable in Africa and Latin America, and less evident in Asia. Rodrik terms this phenomenon

---

[4] In the standard national accounts terminology the term 'industry' encompasses mining, manufacturing, construction, and utilities (electricity, water, and gas). Following the general practice in the literature on development economics we used this term specifically to refer to 'manufacturing'; and the two terms are used interchangeably in the rest of the Element (United Nations 2009).

[5] As Felipe et al. (2015) show using a global data set of manufacturing output and employment for 1970–2010, industrialization in employment is far more important for a country to become rich than industrialization in output, and industrialization, especially in employment, has often preceded a country becoming rich.

'pre-mature de-industrialization' as employment and value added shares in manufacturing are falling in Africa and Latin America at much lower levels of income as compared to the early industrializers (see also Tregenna 2014). Rodrik attributes this phenomenon to globalization and labour-saving technical change. However, Kruse et al. (2021) dispute this finding, using data from the ETD. Similarly, Haraguchi et al. (2017) argue that there is no evidence to support the argument that manufacturing's role in economic development has lessened in the recent decades. Felipe and Mehta (2016) also find that manufacturing's share of global employment did not fall between 1970 and 2010. We return to the issue of whether one can observe a phenomenon of 'premature de-industrialization' in today's low- and middle-income countries in Section 4 of the Element.

A second area of debate is whether services can play the key role in the transformation process instead of manufacturing. With the increasing scepticism of the potential for manufacturing to serve as the driver for economic growth and poverty reduction in the future, there has been interest among scholars and policymakers on whether services can instead play the key role in the structural transformation process in moving a large number of workers out of low productivity jobs in agriculture (Nayyar et al. 2018, 2021). Gollin (2018) argues that the modern services sector has some of the features associated with manufacturing, such as knowledge and technology spill-overs and agglomeration economies. As Gollin notes, 'the service sector has historically taken on many of the beneficial characteristics historically associated with manufacturing' (2018: 3). Similarly, Baldwin and Forslid (2019) argue that with the increasing availability of digital technology which is making remote work possible, many service sectors are becoming more tradable, leading to the possibility that service-led path of economic transformation is a feasible strategy for many low- and middle-income countries. Newfarmer et al. (2018) argue that 'industries without smokestacks' – agro-processing and horticulture, tourism, business, and trading services – can provide a large number of high-productivity jobs, especially in sub-Saharan Africa, where manufacturing has not shown the same dynamism as in East Asia.

It is important to recognize here that services sector in low-income countries is of two types – one, that is highly productive, mostly comprising the business services sector (information and communication technology and finance); and the other, that is relatively low productivity, mostly comprising the non-business services sector (e.g., trade, hotels and restaurants, and the public sector). As we will see later, this distinction is important in our understanding of the process of structural transformation – treating the service sector in a monolithic manner does not take into account the difference in the roles that business and non-business services play in structural transformation – and for the rest of the Element, we will disaggregate the service sector into business services and non-business services, when it makes sense to do so.[6] We will examine to what extent business services have played a key role in the process of structural transformation for low- and middle-income countries, as compared to non-business services, in this Element.

Drivers of Structural Transformation

What are the determinants of structural transformation? What explains why some countries are better able to move workers out of agriculture to manufacturing than others? Why do we see the hump-shaped nature of manufacturing employment and output share as per capita incomes rise? In recent years, after a long lull, there has been an explosion of research on our theoretical understanding of the drivers of structural transformation, especially in the mainstream tradition. We first review the theoretical approaches to structural transformation in Section 2. Two main drivers have been pointed out in the literature – sectoral productivity growth differentials and demand composition effects. More recent work has highlighted the role of globalization and sectoral input–output linkages. We assess the empirical validity of the postulated drivers of structural transformation using the ETD data in Section 5.

Structural Transformation and Inequality

While structural transformation is an essential feature of rapid and sustained growth, since Kuznets's seminal (1955) piece, it is widely believed that structural transformation can lead to higher inequality, at least initially. Therefore, rapid structural transformation may entail a trade-off between growth and inequality, which may be called the developer's dilemma (Alisjahbana et al. 2022). As Kuznets argued, while inequality may increase at the early stages of structural transformation, beyond a certain level of structural transformation, inequality will decrease, giving rise to the famous inverted U-shaped relationship between income and inequality – the so-called Kuznets curve. In this Element, we evaluate the argument that structural transformation may cause

---

[6] As Nayyar (2019) argues, non-business service sectors such as wholesale and retail trade, hotels, and restaurants, or social, community and personal services are essentially unskilled labour-intensive with low entry barriers and low technological levels for service provision. In contrast, business services sectors communication services, financial services, business services, and real estate services are skill-intensive or human capital–intensive, high barriers to entry, and high technological levels for service provision. A large proportion of the non-business service sector is informally employed, while a large proportion of the business services sector is formally employed.

increases in inequality in the early stage of the development process, using data from ETD and the World Income Inequality Data-base (WIID). We do this in Section 6.

Structure of the Element

The rest of the Element has six sections. In Section 2, we review the main theoretical approaches to structural transformation, making a distinction between the classical and neoclassical approaches to structural transformation. We review both the earlier literature and the more recent literature. In Section 3, we introduce the Economic Transformation Database (ETD), discuss its advantages over other available data sets, and propose the typology of structural transformation that we will use in the Element. In Section 4, we set out the patterns of structural transformation, using our typology. In Section 5, we assess the empirical basis for the drivers of structural transformation proposed in the theoretical literature. In Section 6, we examine the relationship between structural transformation, inequality, and poverty. Section 7 concludes with some policy implications that follow from the analysis presented in the Element.

2 Theories of Structural Transformation

Why is the movement of workers from agriculture to manufacturing and services related to economic growth and development? What explains this movement, and why do we see differences in country experiences with structural transformation? A large literature has emerged which attempts to address these core questions in structural transformation through the lens of theory. The two broad theoretical approaches in the literature are the classical and the neoclassical approaches. In this section, we briefly review the classical and neoclassical theoretical approaches to structural transformation.

2.1 The Classical Approach to Structural Transformation

A key feature of the classical approach was the recognition that the overall transformation of demand, trade, production, and employment was the central feature of economic development (Chenery 1988). The emphasis on economic structure and differences that may exist in productivity and other economic characteristics across sectors differentiated the classical from the neoclassical approach of the 1950s, which assumed steady state or balanced growth scenarios (Syrquin 1988).

A fundamental assumption of the classical approach was differences in factor returns that one may observe across economic sectors was not temporary, and could be long-lasting. Therefore, 'in the absence of a continuous equalisation of factor returns across sectors, the reallocation of resources to sectors of higher productivity growth becomes a potential source of growth if it leads to a fuller or better utilization of resources' (Syrquin 1988: 208). Further, 'the potential gains are likely to be more important for developing countries than developed countries since the former exhibit more pronounced symptoms of disequilibrium and can achieve faster rates of structural change' (Syrquin 1988: 208–209). Thus, the classical approach had at its core a model of the economy which was a dual economy and where economic development was inherently a process of disequilibrium.

The two key components of the classical approach was capital accumulation in the modern sector and sectoral composition of output and employment. The former necessitated an aggregative approach, while the latter is, by its nature, at a disaggregated level but in an economy-wide framework. As Syrquin (1988: 211) states, 'accelerating and sustaining growth required increasing the rates of accumulation and maintaining sectoral balance to prevent disequilibrium in product markets, or to overcome disequilibrium prevailing in factor markets'. Therefore, in the classical approach, increases in the investment rate was seen as fundamental in increasing economic growth. As Lewis (1954: 155) notes, 'the central problem in the theory of economic development is to understand the process by which a community which was previously saving and investing 4 or 5 per cent of its national income or less, converts itself into an economy where voluntary saving is running at about 12 or 15 per cent of national income or more'.

In addition to capital formation, classical theories of structural transformation stressed sectoral differences and the dualistic nature of the economies of developing countries. The sectoral differences took different forms in the works of the classical economists. For example, Colin Clark (1940) took the sectors as primary-secondary-tertiary. The Nobel Laureate W. Arthur Lewis took the sectors as traditional-modern, where the traditional-modern did not correspond entirely to the agriculture-manufacturing/services dichotomy which has now become standard in the modern literature on structural transformation (Gollin 2014) since commercial agriculture could be considered as part of the 'modern' sector, and that there may be parts of the services sector such as petty retail trading which could be considered as 'traditional'.

Among the classical economists, the clearest theoretical exposition of how structural transformation occurs, and how this may be related to economic growth, is provided by Lewis. For Lewis, the difference between the traditional and modern sectors is that in the former sector, there is a large mass of under-employed workers, with low productivity, while in the modern sector, productivity is high and capitalist methods of production are used. As Lewis (1954: 147) notes, productivity is high in this sector as it is 'fructified by capital'. Economic growth will occur with the expansion of the modern sector as workers move out of the low-productivity traditional sector to the modern sector. The expansion required an increase in savings which can only come from the capitalist sector or from external sources (Gollin 2014). With capital accumulation, jobs are created in the modern sector, which are filled by workers from the traditional sector. As these workers move, the savings rate of the economy rises, leading to a virtuous circle that steadily raises the level of income per worker in the economy.

How does structural transformation occur in the Lewis model? We now provide a simple exposition of the Lewis model.[7] In the standard Lewisian framework, the increase in employment in the modern/ capitalist sector occurs due to a rightward shift in the demand for labour curve in that sector (Lewis 1954). Though Lewis defined the modern/capitalist sector broadly to include any activity characterized by modern production techniques or with high levels of capital intensity (such as mining, utilities, and plantation agriculture),[8] we will focus our analysis on the manufacturing sector, which is the sector most capable of all Lewis characterized as being in the capitalist sector of generating jobs of a sufficient scale (Fields 2004). Due to a wage gap between the manufacturing and the agricultural sectors (the subsistence sector, in Lewis's original framework), where the manufacturing wage rate is higher than the subsistence wage in the agricultural sector, surplus labour moves from the agricultural sector to the manufacturing sector (Basu 1989). In Lewis's model, the wage rate in the manufacturing sector is institutionally set (Fields 2004). The wage rate in the agricultural sector, on the other hand, is set in relation to the average productivity in that sector. As long as the real wage differential between the manufacturing and agricultural sectors is sufficiently large, firms in the manufacturing sector will face an unlimited supply of labour from the agricultural sector – that is, they can hire as many workers as they want without increasing the manufacturing wage rate. As the demand for labour in the manufacturing sector shifts rightwards, the labour force in the agricultural sector diminishes, increasing the agricultural wage rate. This movement of labour from the agricultural to the manufacturing sector at the institutionally

---

[7] An important extension of the Lewis model is the one proposed by Ranis and Fei (1961), which brought in more explicitly the role of agricultural growth in the structural transformation process.

[8] As Lewis (1954) noted, 'what we have is not one island of expanding capitalist employment, surrounded by a sea of subsistence, but rather a number of such tiny islands. We find a few industries highly capitalized, such as mining or electric power side by side with the most primitive techniques; a few high class shops, surrounded by masses of old style traders; a few capitalized plantations, surrounded by a sea of peasants' (p. 147).

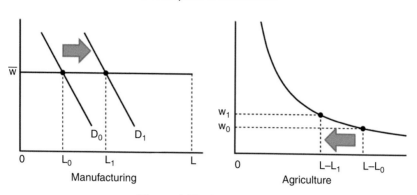

Figure 1 The Lewis model
Source: author's illustration.

set fixed manufacturing wage rate will come to an end when the agricultural wage rises to the level of the manufacturing wage rate.

We next provide a simple graphical depiction of the Lewis model. We depict the movement of labour from the agricultural to the manufacturing sector in Figure 1. The demand for labour curve is denoted by D, and employment is denoted by L. The wage rate in the manufacturing sector is set at $\overline{w}$. With a shift rightwards of the demand for labour curve from D_0 to D_1, employment in the manufacturing sector increases from L_0 to L_1. Agricultural wages increase from w_0 to w_1 as labour exits from the agricultural sector, leading to a fall in employment in the agricultural sector from $L-L_0$ to $L-L_1$.

What explains the rightward shift in the demand for labour curve? Implicitly, in the Lewisian framework, this is because of an increase in manufacturing output. This could occur through investment and accumulation as capitalists re-invest their profits (Lewis 1954). We depict this possibility in Figure 2. To see how output would affect the demand for labour, we draw a line that gives the different levels of labour demanded at different levels of output in the upper panel of the figure. As output increases from Q_0 to Q_1, labour demand increases from D_0 to D_1, leading to higher employment in the manufacturing sector (L_0 to L_1) at a given real wage (shown in the lower panel of Figure 2). Therefore, as long as there was surplus labour in the agricultural sector, structural transformation (i.e., the movement of workers from agriculture to manufacturing) would be associated with economic growth and higher average productivity in the economy.[9]

---

[9] Implicit in the Lewis model is the assumption that strong manufacturing output growth will necessarily lead to large employment creation in the manufacturing sector – the so-called scale effect. Sen (2019a) argues that the extent of employment creation in manufacturing will also depend on two other effects – firstly, whether the increase in manufacturing output occurs mostly in the labour-intensive industries relative to capital intensive industries; and secondly, whether the increase in manufacturing output is mostly due to an increase in labour productivity (or a fall in

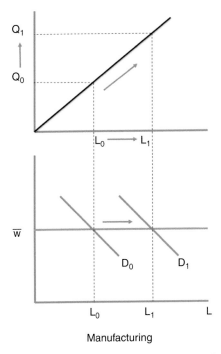

Figure 2 Structural transformation in the Lewis model

Source: author's illustration.

Lewis did not provide a clear theoretical answer on why we may see different rates of structural transformation across countries. While Clark (1940)'s approach is mostly empirical, he did relate the observed shifts in employment and production structures to differential productivity growth across sectors and shifts in demand over time. As Clark (1940, p. 204) argues, sectoral re-allocation of resources can be

> fully explained in terms of two causes, and in terms of them alone. The first is the relative changes in demand on the part of consumers for different types of goods and services ... The second cause is quite different and independent. Over a time when consumers' demands are not changing at all, it is possible that output for worker may be increasing more rapidly in some forms of production than in others; under these circumstances, there will be a transfer

labour intensity of production), which would mute the effect of manufacturing output growth on employment creation. The first effect can be called the composition effect, and the second effect can be called the labour intensity effect. Sen shows that whether an increase in the size of the manufacturing sector has a large effect on job creation would depend on the relative strengths of the three effects, and whether they are in the same direction (the scale effect would always be positive, the composition and labour intensity effects not necessarily so).

of labour away from those industries where output for worker is increasing more rapidly (or decreasing less rapidly).

Clark's explanation of the twin causes of structural transformation – relative sectoral productivity growth differences and Engel effects related to changes in demand – became the mainstay of the neoclassical approach to structural transformation, which we turn to next.

2.2 The Neoclassical Approach to Structural Transformation

The workhorse model of economic growth in the neoclassical tradition is the Solow–Swan model. This model was proposed independently by Robert Solow and Trevor Swan in 1956. The model economy had one sector, where a single good was produced using two factors of production – capital and labour. Capital was subject to diminishing returns, and the rate of technological progress was taken as exogenous. The model predicts that in the long run, economies converge to their steady state equilibrium and that permanent growth is achievable only through technological progress. Thus, by its very nature, the Solow–Swan model abstracted from sectoral allocation issues in the process of economic development, focusing on the role of capital accumulation and technological change in the aggregate. As Herrendorf, Rogerson, and Valentinyi (henceforth, HRV 2014) note:

> The one–sector growth model has become the workhorse of modern macroeconomics. The popularity of the one–sector growth model is at least partly due to the fact that it captures in a minimalist fashion the essence of modern economic growth, which Kuznets (1973) in his Nobel prize lecture described as the sustained increase in productivity and living standards. By virtue of being a minimalist structure, the one–sector growth model necessarily abstracts from several features of the process of economic growth. One of these is the process of structural transformation, that is, the reallocation of economic activity across the broad sectors agriculture, manufacturing and services. (p. 855)

The limitation of the neoclassical approach (until recently) to explain structural transformation was noted as early as 1988 by Moses Syrquin. As Syrquin (1988: 211) notes, 'in the aggregative version (of the neoclassical approach), there is no surplus labour and long-run growth is independent of the savings rate. In multi-sectoral models of the von-Neumann type, growth, still independent of the savings rate, proceeds in a balanced fashion and no disequilibrium is allowed'.

The emphasis on balanced growth has been a cornerstone of neoclassical growth for a long time. Balanced growth models could reproduce the so-called Kaldor stylized facts of growth: the relative constancy of the growth rate, the capital-output ratio, the capital share of income, and the real interest rate (Acemoglu and Guerrieri 2008). However, as HRV (p. 4) note, 'the conditions under which one can simultaneously generate balanced growth and structural transformation are rather limited and that under these conditions, the multi-sectoral model is not able to account for the broad set of empirical regularities that characterize structural transformation'. HRV argue that 'progress in building better models of structural transformation will come from focusing on the forces behind structural transformation without insisting on exact balanced growth' (Acemoglu and Guerrieri 2008, p. 4).

One of the earliest attempts to move away from balanced growth assumptions in the neoclassical framework was that by William Baumol (1967). Baumol emphasized the unbalanced nature of growth due to differential productivity growth across sectors, leading to the famous Baumol thesis: that the relative price of services increases with economic development. Acemoglu and Guerrieri (2008) provide an extension of Baumol's model by allowing for differences in factor proportions across sectors. By doing so, they show that these differences combined with capital deepening leads to non-balanced growth because an increase in the capital output ratio increases output more in sectors with greater capital intensity. Their model can deliver non-balanced growth at the sectoral level but, at the same time, remain consistent with the Kaldor facts in the long run. The Baumol and Acemoglu–Guerrieri models can be seen as the first credible attempts to incorporate sectoral allocation of resources in neoclassical models of economic growth.

Since the early 2000s, a series of path-breaking papers were developed of multisector models of growth in the neoclassical tradition that were consistent with the stylized facts of structural transformation, such as Ngai and Pissarides (2007), Rogerson (2007), Duarte and Restuccia (2010), and Herrendorf, Rogerson, and Valentinyi (2014). Consistent with the neoclassical approach, the models assumed utility maximization by households and profit maximization by producers in the different sectors. Initially, two classes of models were developed: (i) one where the causal explanation was technological or supply-side in nature and which attributed structural transformation to different rates of sectoral total factor productivity growth, and (ii) the second, which was a utility-based or demand-side explanation that required different income elasticities for different goods and could yield structural transformation even with equal total factor productivity growth across all sectors. However, these models assumed a closed economy and also paid less attention to input–output linkages. More recently, there has been attempts to incorporate open economy considerations and construct models which explicitly bring in input–output linkages in the economy. We will first describe the supply-side and demand-side classes of neoclassical models, then briefly discuss the recent theoretical developments in the neoclassical approach to structural transformation.

Supply-Side Models of Structural Transformation

A pioneering paper by Ngai and Pissarides (2007) derived the implications of differential sectoral total factor productivity (TFP) growth rates for structural transformation. Using a benchmark model of many consumption goods and one capital good and with identical production functions across sectors, Ngai-Pissarides show that with low elasticity of substitution across final goods, differences in sectoral TFP growth rates lead to shifts of employment to sectors with low TFP growth through changes in relative prices. Therefore, if TFP growth is higher in agriculture than in services (with TFP growth in manufacturing somewhere in between), relative prices fall in agriculture as compared to services, leading to a re-allocation of workers from agriculture to services. Ngai-Pissarides show that manufacturing's employment share will be either monotonically decreasing or hump-shaped.

More recent supply-side models of structural transformation have been proposed by Fujiwara and Matsuyama (2020), Huneeus and Rogerson (2020), and Sposi et al. (2021) to capture an important stylized fact of structural transformation that we have noted in Section 1 – the phenomenon of premature deindustrialization. Huneeus and Rogerson show that productivity growth in agriculture leads to an increase in the manufacturing employment share, and productivity growth in the non-agricultural sector leads to a flow of workers out of manufacturing under empirically reasonable specifications. At low levels of development, the first force dominates, and at higher levels of development, the second force dominates. This generates the inverse U-shaped nature of manufacturing employment share as income increases. The reason why some countries see manufacturing employment share peaking earlier than others is that sectoral productivity growth rates differ across countries. For countries with slower agricultural productivity growth relative to the rest of the world, manufacturing employment share will peak at a lower level and at an earlier point in the development process. Huneeus and Rogerson argue that differences in agricultural productivity rates across countries can account for the majority of the variation in peak employment shares. The fact that agricultural productivity differs greatly across countries and is particularly low in sub-Saharan Africa has been observed by several scholars, including by Gollin et al. (2014), and may explain the possibility that sub-Saharan African countries are witnessing the phenomenon of premature deindustrialization. However, as we will argue in Section 5, when we look at the drivers of structural transformation, it is not clear whether sectoral productivity growth differences can explain the patterns of structural transformation that we see in the data, especially for low-income countries.

The models proposed by Fujiwara and Matsuyama (2020), and Sposi et al. (2021), also look at differences in sectoral productivity growth to explain the phenomenon of deindustrialization. In Fujiwara-Matsuyama, countries differ in their ability to adopt 'frontier technology', and premature deindustrialization occurs if adoption takes longer in the service sector than in the manufacturing and agricultural sectors, and poorer countries with larger technology gaps reach the peak manufacturing employment share later and at a lower level of income than richer countries with smaller technology gaps. Sposi et al. bring in sectoral trade integration along with sector-biased productivity growth and show that this leads to a twin phenomenon of deindustrialization and increasing industry polarization.

Demand-Side Models of Structural Transformation

Demand-side models of structural transformation highlight the role of differences in sectoral income elasticities in explaining sectoral re-allocation of labour. If relative sectoral demand shows a strong and stable dependence on income, changes in income will lead to a re-allocation of resources towards sectors with higher income elasticities. For example, if there is a falling demand for agricultural goods and an increasing demand for services with increases in income this would give rise to sizeable shifts of workers from agriculture to services when both sectors are compared to manufacturing. An earlier class of demand-side models (such as Kongsamut et al. 2001) relied on specific classes of utility functions with non-homothetic preferences such as generalized Stone-Geary preferences to generate Engel effects on sectoral demand and consequently, changes in sectoral employment and production.

However, a limitation of such models is that they imply that the slopes of relative Engel curves flatten out rapidly over time. Consequently, these models have limited explanatory power in explaining structural transformation in the long run. Comin et al. (2021) provide a model which assumes non-homothetic Constant of Elasticity (CES) preferences. The advantage of using such a class of utility functions is that they can generate non-homothetic sectoral demand for all levels of incomes, and sectoral Engel curves do not level off with increases in income. Using such a class of utility functions, Comin et al. show that demand-side factors can play a larger role in explaining structural transformation than has been accounted for by previous studies.

In Annexe A1, we propose a simple formal neoclassical model of structural transformation that combines demand- and supply-side explanations, and then assess whether the model is able to replicate the patterns of structural transformation that we observe in the ETD data.

Recent Developments in the Neoclassical Approach to Structural Transformation

Two recent classes of neoclassical models have been developed to take into account key limitations of the earlier models of structural transformation. One limitation is that these models are mostly of the closed economy and do not incorporate the fact that in the current economic environment, most economies are well integrated with the rest of the world (Rodrik 2016). A second limitation is that the earlier models assume away cross-sectoral input–output relationships, when both recent theoretical and empirical research suggest that input–output relationships matter for aggregate total factor productivity and output (Valentinyi 2021). We briefly discuss these recent developments in the neoclassical approach to structural transformation.

We first discuss the extensions of the closed economy neoclassical models of structural transformation to the open economy. As Matsuyama (2009: 478) notes,

> we live in the global economy where economies are interdependent with one another. Most empirical studies of structural change, however, write down a closed economy model, apply it to each country, and use the cross-country data to test the model. Effectively, they treat each country as an autarky as if these countries were still isolated fiefdoms in the Middle Ages or were located on different planets.

Matysuyama further argues that assuming that economies are closed would imply that with productivity growth in manufacturing, say in a country like South Korea, the supply-side approach to structural transformation would predict that the number of workers in manufacturing in South Korea would fall. However, since South Korea has significant trade in manufacturing with the rest of the world, the displacement of workers in manufacturing may not occur in South Korea, but in countries that South Korea trades with such as the United States or the UK.

Matsuyama proposes a simple two-economy Ricardian model of trade and structural change, and shows that with trade, productivity growth in manufacturing in the home economy can lead to two countervailing effects – first, an income effect, where manufacturing employment falls at home; and the second, a trade effect, where manufacturing employment increases at home. This suggests that closed economy supply-side models of structural transformation may yield incorrect predictions which are not consistent with empirical facts (since countries with high productivity growth in manufacturing as in East Asia have witnessed increases in manufacturing employment share).[10]

In a similar vein, Rodrik (2016) proposes a model of structural change with international trade and labour-saving technological progress, and uses the model to characterize scenarios where the home country is an advanced economy, a developing economy with comparative advantage in manufacturing, and a developing economy without such a comparative advantage. The model predicts that (a) for the advanced economy, manufacturing employment will sharply decline with the impact on manufacturing output depending on the net effect of technology (positive) and trade (negative), (b) for the developing economy with comparative advantage in manufacturing, there will be an increase in manufacturing output (and possibly employment), and (c) for the developing economy without comparative advantage in manufacturing, there will be a decrease in manufacturing output and employment.[11]

A limitation of the earlier neoclassical models of structural transformation was that they did not pay sufficient attention to the increasing importance of global value chains (GVCs) or global production networks in world trade, where firms in a sector of one country ship intermediate inputs to firms in other sectors based in another country for production (World Bank 2020; Valentinyi 2021).[12] This is also known as vertical specialization in the literature. As the World Bank (2020: 3) points out, 'GVCs are associated with structural transformation in developing countries, drawing people out of less productive activities and into more productive manufacturing and services activities.' Typically, analysis of structural transformation is based on the use of value-added production functions which assume away cross-sectoral input–output relations (Valentinyi 2021). More recently, models of structural transformation have been developed which incorporate cross-country differences in sectoral linkages or intermediate input intensities across countries. One such model is

---

[10] An alternate explanation of structural change using a trade-theoretic framework is provided by Wood (2017), who argues that the decline in manufacturing employment shares in Africa and Latin America and the increase in manufacturing employment shares in Asia can be explained in part by the fact that Africa and Latin America are land-abundant and Asia is land-scarce. This would be consistent with the predictions of an augmented Heckscher-Ohlin model, as Wood shows.

[11] While the above models focus on manufacturing trade, Lewis et al. (2022) propose a model which includes services trade, and shows that higher-income countries gain relatively more by reducing services trade costs than reducing goods trade costs.

[12] Global value chains break up the production process across countries, with firms in one country specializing in a specific task and not producing the whole product, which may be produced in another country. Global value chains now constitute around 50 per cent of world trade (World Bank 2020).

the one proposed by Sposi (2019) which builds a multi-country general equilibrium model of structural change and calibrate the model to forty-one countries using data from the World Input-Output Database. The model captures the two mechanisms by which sectoral linkages matter for structural transformation. Firstly, differences in sectoral linkages result in asymmetric responses in the composition of value added to otherwise identical changes in the composition of final demand. Secondly, cross-country differences in sectoral linkages result in asymmetric responses of relative prices to otherwise identical changes in productivity. Sposi (2019) show that inter-sectoral linkages operating through these two mechanisms are able to explain the hump-shaped nature of manufacturing output share with increases in per capita income.[13]

What is the empirical evidence of greater vertical specialization on productivity and employment growth in developing countries? Using an unbalanced panel of ninety-one countries over 1970–2013, and measuring vertical specialization using the import content of exports, Pahl and Timmer (2019) find that greater GVC participation has a positive effect on productivity growth but not on manufacturing employment growth. This is consistent with the argument of Rodrik (2018) that the spread of GVCs has had the effect of homogenizing new labour-saving technologies around the world. These new technologies are biased towards skill and other capabilities and away from unskilled labour, making it difficult for low-income countries (who have an abundant supply of unskilled labour) to compete in world markets. However, the Pahl-Timmer study does not directly study the effect of GVC trade or vertical specialization on structural transformation, and this is an area of research that remains to be explored.[14]

2.3 Concluding Remarks

The classical approach to economic development was built on the premise that economic growth was deeply interrelated with processes of structural transformation. The classical approach took as its starting point that economic growth was a disequilibrium process and involved the movement of workers and economic activity from low-productivity traditional sectors such as agriculture to high-productivity modern sectors such as manufacturing, and that this movement was driven in large part by capital accumulation in the modern sector. From the 1950s onwards, with the dominance of the one-sector

---

[13] In another recent contribution, Duarte and Restuccia (2020) use a multisector development accounting framework with an input-output structure to explore the implications of heterogeneity in the services sector.

[14] An alternate heterodox perspective on structural change is provided by Alcorta et al. (2021). The analysis here is more in line with the classical approach to structural transformation.

neoclassical model of economic growth in the literature, there was a long period of time when mainstream economists lost interest in issues around structural transformation (though this interest remained strong among the heterodox economists).

More recently, there has been a resurgence of interest among neoclassical economists on what explains the patterns of structural transformation and the different experiences of industrialization that we observe around the world. Interesting and innovative models of structural transformation have been proposed in the theoretical literature. These models in large part formalize the insights of a classical economist, Colin Clark, on the role that demand and supply-side factors play in determining the pace of structural transformation. While the earlier models were mostly of the closed economy variety and did not incorporate important recent trends in the global economy such as the increasing importance of global production networks, more recent developments in the literature bring in open economy considerations and inter-sectoral linkages in production. It could be argued that these models do not fully capture a characteristic of low-income economies, which is the presence of surplus labour in agriculture. More theoretical work needs to be done to develop models that are more in line with the empirical features of low-income countries. Nevertheless, given the impressive work that has occurred in the literature on the modelling of structural transformation, one can be optimistic that this will be the next stage in the theoretical literature of structural transformation in the neoclassical tradition.

3 A Typology of Stages of Structural Transformation

In this section, we first describe the data that we use in the empirical analysis. We then introduce the typology that we will use to study the paths of structural transformation across countries.

3.1 Data

A key challenge that researchers faced in examining patterns of structural transformation in the developing world was the lack of reliable data on sectoral employment and value-added that is comparable across countries and over time. Much of the previous research on structural transformation used the GGDC ten-sector database (e.g., Timmer and de Vries 2009; Duarte and Restuccia 2010; Herrendorf et al. 2014; Diao et al. 2017). The ten-sector database consists of sectoral and aggregate employment and real value-added statistics for thirty developing countries and nine high-income countries covering the period up to 2010 and, for some countries, to 2011 or 2012. A strength of the database was that the sectoral employment is obtained from the population censuses which have a more complete coverage of informal employment as compared to the labour force surveys. Therefore, employment data in the ten-sector database can be taken to broadly coincide with actual employment levels, regardless of formality status (Diao et al. 2017). Furthermore, GGDC has specialized in providing harmonized and consistent data on sectoral real-value added, which provides a significant amount of credibility to the data. However, an important limitation of the ten-sector database is that it has only two low-income countries – Ethiopia and Malawi.[15] In addition, the data end in 2010 for most countries, when the period following 2010 has seen quite remarkable shifts in sectoral patterns in employment and value added, especially in sub-Saharan Africa (see Kruse et al. 2021).

In the analysis of structural transformation in this monograph, we use the newly launched GGDC/UNU-WIDER Economic Transformation Database (ETD). The ETD provides time-series of employment and real and nominal value added by twelve sectors in fifty-one countries for the period 1990–2018. It includes twenty Asian, nine Latin American, four Middle East and North African (MENA), and eighteen sub-Saharan African countries/economies at varying levels of economic development. The ETD is constructed from an in-depth investigation of the availability and usability of statistical sources on a country-by-country basis. The ETD is a new data set; it is not an update of time series in an existing sectoral data set. In comparison to the GGDC ten-sector database (Timmer and de Vries 2009), the ETD has better coverage of low-income developing countries, distinguishes twelve sectors in the ISIC revision 4 classification, and has time-series data that run until 2018.

Table 1 gives an overview of the content of the ETD. The data set consists of fifty-one countries at varying levels of economic development. It includes twenty Asian, nine Latin American, four Middle-Eastern and North African (MENA), and eighteen sub-Saharan African countries/economies.[16] According to data for 2018, they account for a major part of the output of each region, namely 98 per cent, 82 per cent, 36 per cent, and 73 per cent of GDP in Asia, Latin America, MENA, and sub-Saharan Africa, respectively. The ETD countries account for 55 per cent of global real manufacturing VA and 42 per cent of global GDP. The database is constructed by an in-depth investigation of the availability and usability of statistical sources on a country-by-country basis. See de Vries et al. (2021) for a detailed documentation of the sources and methods.

---

[15] Using the World Bank's definition of low-income countries in 2019–2020.

[16] Comparable data for North American and European countries are available at www.euklems.eu. Asian countries are grouped into developing Asia based on the classification by the IMF (2018).

Table 1 Content of GGDC/UNU-WIDER Economic Transformation Database

Countries included:	
Developing Asia (14)	Bangladesh, Cambodia, China, India, Indonesia, Lao People's Democratic Republic, Malaysia, Myanmar, Nepal, Pakistan, Philippines, Sri Lanka, Thailand, Viet Nam
Advanced Asia (6)	Hong Kong (China), Israel, Japan, Korea (Rep. of), Singapore, Chinese Taipei
Latin America (9)	Argentina, Bolivia, Brazil, Chile, Colombia, Costa Rica, Ecuador, Mexico, Peru
Middle East and North Africa (4)	Egypt, Morocco, Tunisia, Turkey
Sub-Saharan Africa (18)	Botswana, Burkina Faso, Cameroon, Ethiopia, Ghana, Kenya, Lesotho, Malawi, Mauritius, Mozambique, Namibia, Nigeria, Rwanda, Senegal, South Africa, Tanzania, Uganda, Zambia
# of sectors	*Brief description (ISIC rev. 4)*
1.	Agriculture (A)
2.	Mining (B)
3.	Manufacturing (C)
4.	Utilities (D+E)
5.	Construction (F)
6.	Trade services (G + I)
7.	Transport services (H)
8.	Business services (J + M + N)
9.	Financial services (K)
10.	Real estate (L)
11.	Government services (O + P + Q)
12.	Other services (R + S + T + U)
Time period (annual)	1990 – 2018
Variables	Gross value added at constant (2015) prices (national currency in millions)
	Gross value added at current prices (national currency in millions)
	Persons employed (in thousands)
Principal sources	National accounts; population censuses; labour force surveys; business surveys
Available at:	GGDC and UNU-WIDER, public release 17 February 2021

Source: author's calculations.

The ETD includes annual data on gross value added at both real and nominal prices for the period 1990–2018. Data on persons employed are also included such that labour productivity (value added per worker) trends can be derived. The database covers the twelve main sectors of the economy as defined in the International Standard Industrial Classification, revision 4 (ISIC rev. 4). Together these twelve sectors cover the total economy.

The data on gross value added in real and nominal prices are from the National Accounts published by the National Statistical Institutes, which accounts for income from formal and informal activities.[17] Employment in the ETD is defined as 'all persons engaged', thus including all paid employees, but also self-employed and family workers, with an age boundary of fifteen years and older. Hence, it aims to include formal and informal workers. Ideally, labour input is measured in hours worked, as differences in hours worked across sectors affect sectoral productivity gaps (Gollin et al. 2014). However, the data, insofar available, are irregular, and information on hours worked typically only covers the formal sector (see Kruse et al. 2021).[18]

The ETD is not the only database that provides sectoral data on value added and employment. For example, the World Bank's World Development Indicators (WDI) provide value-added database on national accounts data and are, therefore, comparable. For employment, the ILO provides sectoral data. However, the ETD is superior to the ILO's employment data in several ways. Firstly, while the ETD prefers population censuses, the ILO model prioritizes labour force surveys. Sometimes LFS are not nationally representative and cover urban agglomerations only. As a result, sectoral employment shares can be unreliable.[19] Another major difference is the reliance on econometric

---

[17] Note that the value added from real estate activities (ISIC rev 4 industry L) consists of value added from rental activities and imputations of owner-occupied housing. The latter imputation is based on an equivalent rent approach and is added to GDP. Imputed income from dwellings does not have an employment equivalent and therefore it is preferably excluded in productivity analysis. This is possible, because real estate activities are separately reported in the ETD.

[18] Whenever appropriate, population censuses are used to indicate absolute levels of employment, and LFS and business surveys are used to indicate trends in between. For countries where population data are not used, nationally representative labour force surveys are used as benchmarks instead. If employment series are not available to measure trends between benchmarks, the interpolation between benchmarks is based on the ILO model-based sectoral employment trends or the average trends in labour productivity between benchmark years for non-agricultural sectors. Employment in agriculture is interpolated between benchmarks using series of the economically active population in agriculture (see de Vries et al. 2021 for further information).

[19] Urban labour force surveys are not representative of the sectoral employment structure in most economies. In particular, if such surveys are used, it may provide unreliable employment estimates in agriculture. For example, in 2010 the agricultural employment share for Argentina in the ILO model-based data set is 1.3 per cent of the workforce (ilostat.ilo.org accessed September 2020), which compares with a population census–based estimate of 6.0 per cent in the ETD for that year. In the ILO data set, the agricultural share drops to

imputation methods to fill up blanks in the ILO model (see Kruse et al. 2021 for further details).

Secondly, and most importantly, at the 19th International Conference of Labour Statisticians (ICLS) in 2013 it was decided to narrow the definition of employment to work for pay or profit only. That definition induces a downward effect on the level of agricultural employment, because farmers who mainly or exclusively produce for own use are no longer included in employment by the ILO (Gaddis et al. 2020). Production of agricultural goods for own use falls within the boundaries of the system of national accounts and is therefore included in agricultural value added.[20] Hence, the implementation of the 19th ICLS standards creates an inconsistency between value added in the national accounts and ILO model-based employment estimates for agriculture. This implies that that is difficult to obtain accurate and consistent time series of employment in developing countries using the ICLS definition where subsistence production is common (Klasen 2019) as well as providing misleading information on the sectoral distribution of employment (Gaddis et al. 2020). Currently it is not clear whether, how or for which countries and time periods the 19th ICLS standards have been implemented. The ETD avoids these issues, as it uses the old definition and includes subsistence production workers (Kruse et al. 2021).

The ETD does not contain data on high-income countries (except Japan and South Korea). While in principle, we could merge the GGDC 10 sector database with the ETD to have an unified database on structural transformation for high-income, middle-income, and low-income countries, we do not do this in our empirical analysis for three reasons. The first reason has to do with our conceptual understanding of structural transformation. The second and third reasons have to with constraints of data. On the first reason: high-income countries such as the United Kingdom and the United States have reached an advanced stage of structural transformation, where the movement of workers from agriculture to other sectors is largely complete, with very low shares of employment in agriculture. The focus of our Element is on countries which are *yet to reach this advanced stage of structural transformation*. For this reason, it would be preferable to exclude the mature high-income countries in our analysis of the patterns of structural transformation (we retain Japan and South Korea in

---

0.1 per cent by 2018, whereas it is still 5.1 per cent according to the ETD. This is due to the use of urban labour force surveys by the ILO for Argentina.

[20] National income accounts emphasize the monetary economy, yet an exception is made for production of primary products. The 1993 system of national accounts recommends including non-monetary (i.e., own use) production of primary products, and this recommendation is upheld in the 2008 system of national accounts (Gaddis et al. 2020).

our set of countries as they reached high-income status at a later date). Secondly, the GGDC 10 sector database stops in 2010, and we are keen to analyse the period after 2010, as the 2010s were a period of rapid economic growth, especially in sub-Saharan Africa and South Asia, possibly accompanied by significant shifts in sectoral shares of employment and value added. Finally, the ETD uses a twelve-sector classification in contrast to the ten-sector classification used in the original GGDC database which makes sectoral data not strictly comparable. However, in order to check the robustness of our findings, especially in the econometric analysis, we supplement our analysis of the ETD data with the original GGDC data. At the same time, we exclude the real estate sector from our analysis of structural transformation as this sector generates very few jobs and contributes little to GDP.

3.2 A Typology of Stages of Structural Transformation

An important question that is raised right at the outset when we embark on an analysis of the patterns of structural transformation is the following: Should we treat all countries symmetrically? Are there not country differences in the stages of structural transformation or specific features of countries that should be taken into account? The classical approach to structural transformation recognized this possibility when they categorized countries by size (small versus large countries), trade orientation (export-oriented versus import substitution) and so on (see Syrquin 1988). For example, in their classic book on the paths of development, Chenery and Syrquin (1975) classify countries using the following criteria: (a) whether the country specializes in primary products or industrial goods, (b) whether the country has balanced trade and production, and (c) whether the country's trade regime can be classified as export oriented or characterized by import substitution. While this classification made sense at the time of writing of the 1975 book by Chenery and Syrquin, when a large number of developing countries followed import substituting industrialization and many countries were mainly primary producers with little semblance of non-primary production, such a classification is less relevant in contemporary times when most countries have dismantled their import substitution regime and many developing countries have a large part of their workforce in non-primary activities such as manufacturing and services.

In this study, we propose a simple and intuitive way of classifying countries that takes into account the different stages of structural transformation that they are in. A first set of countries are those where agriculture is still the largest sector in terms of the share of employment in the most recent time period available. In our sample, these countries are Burkina Faso, Bangladesh, Cambodia,

Cameroon, Ethiopia, India, Kenya, Lao PDR, Malawi, Mozambique, Myanmar, Nepal, Nigeria, Pakistan, Rwanda, Tanzania, Uganda, Vietnam, and Zambia. These countries are in Asia and sub-Saharan Africa. We call these countries **structurally underdeveloped**. The next set of countries are where more people are employed in the services sector than agriculture, with agriculture being the second largest sector. These countries are Bolivia, Botswana, China, Colombia, Costa Rica, Ecuador, Egypt, Ghana, Indonesia, Lesotho, Morocco, Namibia, the Philippines, Peru, Senegal, Sri Lanka, Thailand, Turkey, and South Africa. We call them **structurally developing countries**. These countries span all three continents – Africa, Asia, and Latin America.[21] The final set of countries has more people employed in manufacturing sector than agriculture. These countries in the sample are Argentina, Brazil, Chile, Hong Kong, Israel, Japan, Malaysia, Mauritius, Mexico, Singapore, South Korea, Taiwan, and Tunisia. These countries are either in East Asia or in Latin America (with the exception of Mauritius, which is in Africa). We call these countries **structurally developed**.[22] We provide the list of countries by stage of structural transformation in Table 2.[23]

A natural question that arises is whether the classification of countries by stages of structural transformation (ST) maps perfectly to the levels of per capita incomes of these countries. In other words, is it the case that all countries which are structurally underdeveloped poorer than countries which are structurally developing? And are all countries which are structurally developing poorer than countries which are structurally developed? To see if this is the case, we provide a box plot of countries in the three different ST groups by their level of per capita income in Figure 3. We observe that as expected, on average, structurally underdeveloped countries are poorer than structurally developing countries, and structurally developing countries are poorer than structurally developed countries. However, we also note that there are countries in the top quartile of

---

[21] It should be noted that several of countries in the structurally developing group would have been classified as structurally underdeveloped in the beginning of the period of analysis (i.e., 1990). These countries are Bolivia, Botswana, China, Ghana, Indonesia, Morocco, Namibia, the Philippines, Senegal, Thailand, and Turkey.

[22] Countries which would have been classified as structurally developing at the beginning of the period of analysis but which are now structurally developed are Brazil, Chile, Mexico, Malaysia, and Tunisia.

[23] Another conventional way to classify countries is to group them by region (sub-Saharan Africa, South Asia, etc.) (see Kruse et al. 2021). However, classifying countries by region is misleading in our context, as whether a country is in a particular stage of structural transformation may not be necessarily linked to regional characteristics. As is evident from our classification, the structurally underdeveloped group contains both African and Asian countries, and the structurally developing group contains countries from Latin America, Africa, and Asia. Our classificatory approach remains in spirit close to the approach of Chenery-Syrquin, who classified countries, not by regions, but by their economic characteristics.

Table 2 Structural transformation country groups

Structural Transformation Group	
Underdeveloped (19)	Burkina Faso, Bangladesh, Cambodia, Cameroon, Ethiopia, India, Kenya, Laos, Malawi, Myanmar, Mozambique, Nigeria, Nepal, Pakistan, Rwanda, Tanzania, Uganda, Vietnam, Zambia
Developing (19)	Bolivia, Botswana, China, Colombia, Costa Rica, Ecuador, Egypt, Ghana, Indonesia, Sri Lanka, Lesotho, Morocco, Namibia, Peru, Philippines, Senegal, Thailand, Turkey, South Africa
Developed (13)	Argentina, Brazil, Chile, Hong Kong, Israel, Japan, Mauritius, Malaysia, Mexico, Singapore, South Korea Taiwan, Tunisia

Source: author's calculations

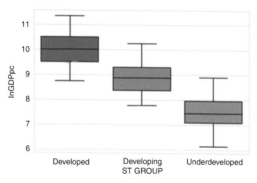

Figure 3 Structural transformation country groups by level of per capita income
Note: ln GDPpc is log of GDP per capita (in constant USD PPP dollars).
Source: author's calculations, using ETD and World Bank's *World Development Indicators*.

incomes in the structurally underdeveloped group which are richer than the bottom two quartiles for the structurally developing group. Similarly, there are countries in the top quartile of the structurally developing group which are richer than the bottom quartile of the structurally developed group. This suggests that per capita income per se is not a reliable marker of a country's progress in structural transformation. That is to say, while high levels of per capita income are a necessary condition to reach higher stages of structural transformation, they are not a sufficient condition.

In Table 3, we provide selected characteristics of the countries in the three structural transformation groups. These characteristics were seen as the 'empirical regularities' accompanying development by Chenery and Syrquin (1975) and Syrquin (1988). Firstly, we note that there is a clear positive relationship between trade structure and stage of structural transformation. Structurally underdeveloped countries have the lowest ratios of exports and manufactured exports as percentages of GDP, followed by structurally developing countries, with structurally developed countries having the most export oriented economies. As already noted, structurally underdeveloped countries are the poorest set of countries, followed by structurally developing countries, with structurally developed countries being the richest. Average GDP per capita in structurally underdeveloped countries is roughly one third of that of structurally developing countries, and average GDP per capita in structurally developing countries are roughly one third that of structurally developed. Interestingly, we do not see a clear positive relationship between investment rates and stage of structural transformation. In fact, structurally developed countries have the lowest investment rates among the three groups of countries. Finally, we note that the structurally underdeveloped and developing countries are much larger in terms of population size than structurally developed countries.

In the next section, we examine the differences in patterns of structural transformation across the three country groups.

4 Patterns of Structural Transformation

In this section, we provide a comprehensive description of the patterns of structural transformation for the fifty-one low- and middle-income countries in Africa, Asia, and Latin America in the ETD database for the period 1990–2018, using the typology introduced in the previous section. In our analysis of the patterns of structural transformation, we focus on employment, value added, and labour productivity.

4.1 Patterns in Sectoral Employment

We begin our descriptive analysis of patterns in sectoral employment by looking at employment shares by disaggregated sectors in all countries in our sample over time (Table 4). The share of agriculture in total employment fell from 47.1 per cent in 1990–94 to 32.0 per cent in 2015–18. There was almost no

Table 3 Selected characteristics by stage of structural transformation (ST), country groups (means)

ST Groups	Exports (% of GDP)	Manufacturing Exports (% of GDP)	Gross Capital Formation (% of GDP)	GDP per capita (PPP, 2017 US$)	Population (millions)
Underdeveloped	26.8	9.1	27.2	3355.4	123.9
	(18.6)	(15.8)	(8.1)	(1565.5)	(281.7)
Developing	31.1	12.9	26.5	11035.7	118.8
	(12.4)	(11.6)	(6.9)	(5050.9)	(315.5)
Developed	62.2	31.3	23.0	32585.7	49.9
	(64.4)	(27.6)	(3.5)	(18550.9)	(61.9)

Note: standard deviations in parentheses.

Source: author's calculations, from World Bank's *World Development Indicators*.

Table 4 Share of employment by stages of structural transformation over time, disaggregated sectors, all countries

Period	Agriculture	Manufacturing Ind.	Non-manufacturing Ind.	Mining	Utilities	Construction	Services	Trade	Transport	Business	Financial	Govt. & Other
1990–94	47.1%	12.0%	6.0%	0.8%	0.6%	4.6%	34.9%	12.7%	3.1%	2.5%	0.9%	15.6%
1995–99	44.6%	11.5%	6.3%	0.7%	0.6%	5.1%	37.6%	14.1%	3.4%	3.1%	1.1%	16.0%
2000–04	41.8%	11.2%	6.2%	0.6%	0.5%	5.1%	40.8%	15.6%	3.6%	3.6%	1.2%	16.7%
2005–09	38.7%	11.1%	6.7%	0.6%	0.5%	5.5%	43.5%	16.8%	4.0%	4.3%	1.3%	17.1%
2010–15	35.3%	11.0%	7.5%	0.8%	0.6%	6.2%	46.3%	17.8%	4.1%	5.0%	1.5%	17.8%
2015–18	32.0%	11.2%	8.0%	0.8%	0.6%	6.7%	48.8%	18.9%	4.3%	5.5%	1.6%	18.4%

Notes: (a) Ind. Is Industry, Serv. Is Services, (b) Non-manufacturing industry is mining, utilities and construction; (c) Services is Trade, Transport, Business, Financial and Govt. and Other.

Source: author's calculations, from ETD.

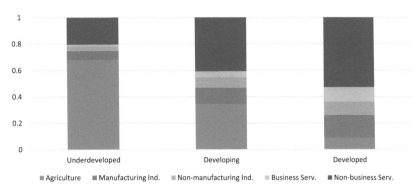

Figure 4 Share of employment by stages of structural transformation
Note: (a) Ind. Is Industry, and Serv. Is Services.
Source: author's calculations, from the ETD data.

change in manufacturing employment share, which was 12 per cent in 1990–94 and 11.2 per cent in 2015–18. There was a small increase in employment share in non-manufacturing industry from 6 per cent in 1990–94 to 8 per cent in 2015–18, due to an increase in employment share in construction. We observe a large increase in the share of employment in services from 34.9 per cent in 1990–94 to 48.8 per cent in 2015–18. This increase in the share of workers in services is also evident in each of the disaggregated sectors, with the largest absolute increase occurring in the trade sub-sector.

In Figure 4, we provide the allocation of workers by stage of structural transformation, averaged over the entire period, 1990–2018. The broad sectors we look at are agriculture, manufacturing industry, non-manufacturing industry (mining, utilities, and construction), business services (including financial services), and non-business services (trade, transport, government, and others). While it is customary to look at sectoral employment by broad categories – agriculture, manufacturing industry, non-manufacturing industry, and services, in our case, we split services into business and non-business services. There are three reasons why we do so. Firstly, as we will show later in this section, the productivity of the business services sector far exceeds that of the non-business services sector, and is comparable to the productivity of the manufacturing sector. Secondly, the business services sector includes the more tradable parts of the services sector (e.g., information technology), while the non-business sector broadly corresponds to the non-tradable services sector. Thirdly, most of the activity that occurs in the business services sector is in enterprises that are in the formal sector (e.g., information technology firms and banks), while a large part of the activity in the non-business services sector is in the informal sector – including self-employed or house-hold enterprises in trade, hotels and restaurants, and personal services (e.g., fruit and vegetable street vendors).[24]

Agriculture provides under 68 per cent of the employment for structurally underdeveloped countries, 34.6 per cent in structurally developing countries, and 8.9 per cent in structurally developed countries. Manufacturing provided an average of 6.6 per cent of employment in structurally underdeveloped countries, 12.1 per cent of employment in structurally developing countries, and 17.2 per cent of employment in structurally developed countries. Non-manufacturing industry (comprising mining, utilities, and construction) provided an average of 3.4 per cent of employment in structurally underdeveloped countries, 7.9 per cent of employment in structurally developing countries, and 10 per cent of employment in structurally developed countries. Business services (including financial services) provided an average of 1.5 per cent of employment in structurally underdeveloped countries, 4.5 per cent of employment in structurally developing countries, and 11.2 per cent of employment in structurally developed countries. Finally, non-business services provided an average of 20.5 per cent of employment in structurally underdeveloped countries, 40.7 per cent of employment in structurally developing countries, and 52.7 per cent of employment in structurally developed countries.

In Table 5, we provide the same information as in Figure 4, except now we do it by sub-decadal sub-periods. We see the very slow movement of workers in agriculture in structurally underdeveloped countries, from 75.5 per cent in 1990–99 to 58.8 per cent in 2010–18. These countries have also seen a slow increase in the share of employment in manufacturing from 5.5 per cent in 1990–99 to around 8.1 per cent in 2010–2018. In the case of structurally developing countries, the average share of employment in services overtakes employment in agriculture only in the 2000s. For these countries, the share of workers in manufacturing actually fell from the period between 1990 and 2018. Nevertheless, these countries have seen rapid decline in the share of employment in agriculture from 42 per cent in 1990–94 to 26 per cent in 2015–18. For structurally developed, the share of employment in agriculture was low to start with at 13 per cent in 1990–94. By the time we reach the period 2015–18, more workers are employed in non-manufacturing industry in these countries than in agriculture, and services at 56 per cent provide the largest employment by far. Here, we observe a fall in the share of employment in manufacturing over time, from 21 per cent in 1990–94 to 14 per cent in 2015–18.

---

[24] The only exception here is the government sector where workers are usually in permanent jobs that are reasonably well-paying.

Table 5 Share of employment by stages of structural transformation over time, by broad sectors and by country group

Country Group	Period	Agriculture	Manufacturing Ind.	Non-manufacturing Ind.	Business Services	Non-Business Services
Underdeveloped	1990–94	77%	5%	2%	1%	15%
Underdeveloped	1995–99	75%	5%	2%	1%	16%
Underdeveloped	2000–04	72%	6%	3%	1%	19%
Underdeveloped	2005–09	67%	7%	3%	2%	22%
Underdeveloped	2010–14	62%	7%	4%	2%	24%
Underdeveloped	2015–18	57%	8%	5%	2%	27%
Developing	1990–94	42%	12%	7%	3%	35%
Developing	1995–99	39%	12%	7%	4%	38%
Developing	2000–04	36%	12%	7%	4%	41%
Developing	2005–09	33%	12%	8%	5%	42%
Developing	2010–14	30%	12%	9%	6%	44%
Developing	2015–18	26%	12%	9%	7%	46%
Developed	1990–94	13%	21%	10%	8%	48%
Developed	1995–99	11%	19%	10%	9%	51%
Developed	2000–04	9%	17%	10%	11%	53%
Developed	2005–09	8%	16%	10%	12%	54%
Developed	2010–14	7%	15%	10%	14%	55%
Developed	2015–18	6%	14%	10%	14%	56%

Notes: (a) Ind. Is Industry, Serv. Is Services; (b) Business Serv. Includes business and financial services; (c) Non-manufacturing Ind. comprises Mining, Utilities, and Construction; (d) Non-business services is Trade, Transport, Government, and Other Services.

Source: author's calculations, from ETD.

It is clear from Table 5 that for structurally underdeveloped economies, most of the growth of employment in the service sector occurs in non-business services rather than business services. This is very different from what is experienced in structurally developing and developed economies, where the most rapid increase in employment for any particular sector is observed in the business services sector; for structurally developing economies, it rises from 3 per cent of total employment in 1990–94 to 7 per cent in 2015–18, and for structurally developed economies, it rises from 8 per cent in 1990–94 to 14 per cent in 2015–18. In contrast, the business services sector remains a paltry 2 per cent of total employment in structurally underdeveloped economies in 2015–18.

The sectoral employment data, by stages of structural transformation, reveal several stylized facts about the patterns of structural transformation, which has also been noted in the previous literature. Firstly, the higher stage of structural transformation, the lower the share of workers in agriculture. Secondly, the lower the stage of structural transformation, the lower the share of workers in manufacturing and non-manufacturing industry. Thirdly, the higher the stage of structural transformation, the higher the share of workers in business and non-business services.

In Section 2, we discussed the Classical approach to structural transformation (as in the work of W. Arthur Lewis), which argued that countries at lower levels of economic development have dualistic labour markets, with large number of workers in the so-called traditional sector, and relatively few workers in the modern sector. We clearly see this feature of economic underdevelopment in the patterns of structural transformation that we observe with the ETD data. If we equate the traditional sector with the agricultural sector, then we see that the largest proportion of workers in the structurally underdeveloped countries are in this sector (around 57 per cent in 2015–18), and with very few workers in the so-called modern sectors – manufacturing industry, non-manufacturing industry, and business services (8, 5, and 2 per cent respectively in 2015–18).[25] In contrast, there is less evidence of such dualism in the structurally developing and structurally developed countries. Clearly, the challenge of economic development for the structurally underdeveloped countries is to move a large proportion of their workers from agriculture to manufacturing, non-manufacturing industry, and business services.

One of the most celebrated findings in the earlier empirical literature on structural transformation is the overall negative relationship between the share of workers in agriculture and level of per capita income (Chenery and Syrquin 1975). Do we find evidence of such a negative relationship even in the more recent period? The answer is unequivocally yes, as is clear from Figure 5. There

---

[25] As noted in Section 2, some parts of non-business services such as trade, hotels, and restaurants share the characteristics of the agricultural sector, in that they are a 'resting place' for surplus labour in the economy.

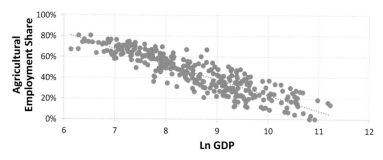

Figure 5 The relationship between agricultural employment share and per capita income, all countries

Note: Ln GDP is natural logarithm of GDP in constant price PPP dollars.

Source: author's calculations, from World Development Indicators and ETD data.

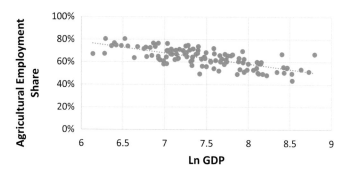

Figure 6 The relationship between agricultural employment share and per capita income, structurally underdeveloped countries

Note: Ln GDP is natural logarithm of GDP in constant price PPP dollars.

Source: author's calculations, from World Development Indicators and ETD data.

is a steady fall in the share of workers in agriculture as countries become richer over time. How does this relationship look if we categorize countries by stages of structural transformation? In Figures 6, 7, and 8, we look at the relationship between agricultural employment share and per capita income by stages of structural transformation. We find that the negative relationship observed for all countries is also evident when we group countries by stages of structural transformation. However, the relationship is weaker for structurally under-developed countries as compared to structurally developing and developed countries, indicating that the movement of workers out of agriculture is much slower for these countries than for countries in higher stages of structural transformation.

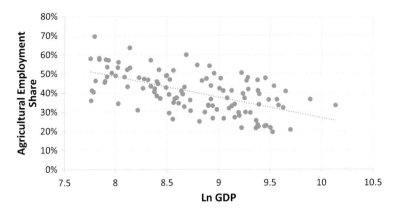

Figure 7 The relationship between agricultural employment share and per capita income, structurally developing countries

Note: Ln GDP is natural logarithm of GDP in constant price PPP dollars.

Source: author's calculations, from World Development Indicators and ETD data.

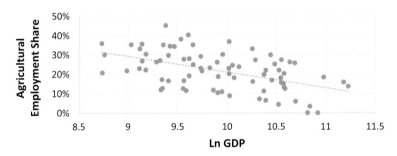

Figure 8 The relationship between agricultural employment share and per capita income, structurally developed countries

Note: Ln GDP is natural logarithm of GDP in constant price PPP dollars.

Source: author's calculations, from World Development Indicators and ETD data.

Figure 9 plots the share of employment in each major sector – agriculture, manufacturing, nonmanufacturing industry, business services, and non-business services – in total employment over time for all countries in our sample. As expected, the share of employment in agriculture falls steadily over time. On the other hand, the share of employment in non-business services shows a steady increase. There is virtually no change in the share of employment in manufacturing industry, non-manufacturing industry, and business services over time.

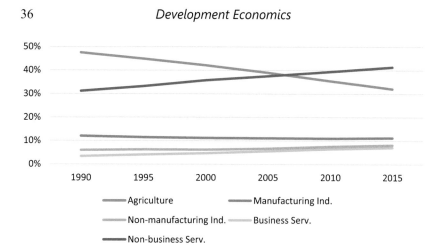

Figure 9 Share of employment by broad sectors over time, all countries
Source: author's calculations, from ETD data.

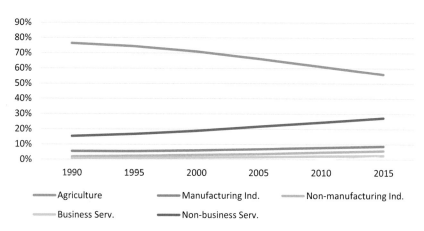

Figure 10 Share of employment by broad sectors over time, structurally
underdeveloped countries
Source: author's calculations, from ETD data.

Figure 10 shows the changes in sectoral employment shares over time for structurally underdeveloped economies. A remarkable feature of structural transformation in these economies is the very slow movement of workers out of agriculture. These workers mostly go to the non-business services sector and not to manufacturing, which shows no clear increase in employment share. The share of employment in business services is very low as well. The share of employment in non-manufacturing industry also shows no clear trend.

Figure 11 shows the changes in sectoral employment shares over time for structurally developing economies. There is a large fall in share of employment

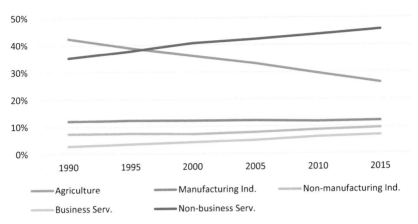

Figure 11 Share of employment by broad sectors, structurally developing countries

Source: author's calculations, from ETD data.

in agriculture for these economies over 1990–2018, from around 42 per cent in 1990–94 to around 26 per cent in 2015–18. This is matched by a corresponding increase in employment in non-business services increases from around 35 per cent to 46 per cent of total employment. Manufacturing employment share remains at around 12 per cent over the entire period. There is an increase in the share of employment in business services, though the percentage of workers in this sector remains quite low at 7 per cent in 2015–18. There is no perceptible change in the share of employment in nonmanufacturing industry.

Figure 12 shows the changes in sectoral employment shares over time for structurally developed economies. The share of employment in agriculture was low to start with in 1990–94 at around 13 per cent period and falls to around 6 per cent by the end of the 2010s. The share of employment in non-business services increases from around 48 per cent to around 56 per cent of total employment. The manufacturing employment share shows a steady decline from 21 per cent in 1990–94 to 14 per cent in 2015–18. Strikingly, the share of employment in business services rises steadily to the point where it has reached the level of the share of manufacturing employment by the end of the 2010s, at 14 per cent. The share of employment in non-manufacturing industry shows no clear trend in 1990–2018.

A striking feature of structural transformation in our fifty-one countries is that the movement of employment from agriculture has been mostly to services (Figure 13). For structurally underdeveloped countries, there has been an increase in the movement of workers away from agriculture since the 1990s till the recent period, which is when several of these countries witnessed fairly

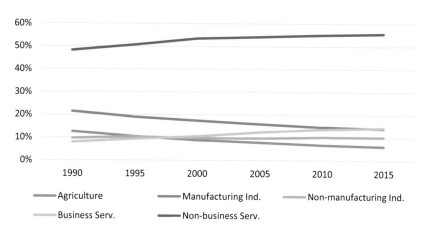

Figure 12 Share of employment by broad sectors, structurally developed countries

Source: author's calculations, from ETD data.

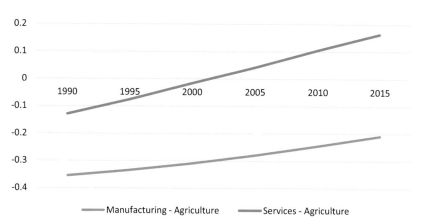

Figure 13 Movement of workers from agriculture to manufacturing and services over time, all countries

Source: author's calculations, from ETD data.

strong growth (Arndt et al. 2016) (Figure 16). We observe a rapid and sustained movement of workers from agriculture to manufacturing and services in structurally developing countries over the entire period (Figure 15). Finally, for structurally developed countries, the movement of workers from agriculture is mostly to services, with the movement of workers from agriculture to manufacturing having stalled by the 1990s (Figure 14).

Would the patterns of structural transformation that we identified in this section look different if we use the more conventionally used income status of the country

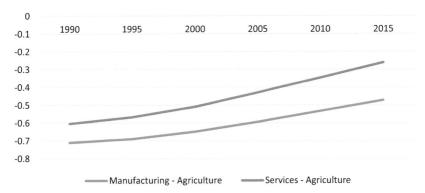

Figure 14 Movement of workers from agriculture to manufacturing and services over time, structurally underdeveloped countries

Source: author's calculations, using ETD data.

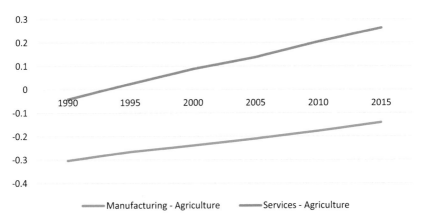

Figure 15 Movement of workers from agriculture to manufacturing and services over time, structurally developing countries

Source: author's calculations, using ETD data.

rather than the stage of structural transformation? We present the sectoral employment shares over time by World Bank income group in Table A1 in the Online Appendix. As is clear from the table, we observe very similar patterns when using income status as compared to stage of structural transformation. Agriculture is the mainstay of employment for low-income countries, while very few workers are in agriculture in high-income countries. Both the shares of business and non-business services are noticeably higher for high-income countries as compared to low-income and low-middle-income countries. Interestingly, the share of manufacturing employment is not noticeably different for low-middle, high-middle, and high-income countries. More than manufacturing employment share, it is the much

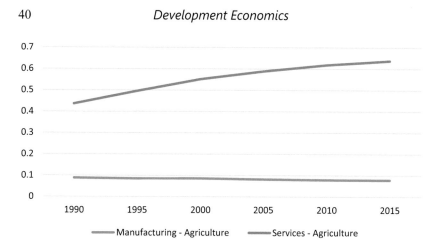

Figure 16 Movement of workers from agriculture to manufacturing and services over time, structurally developed countries

Source: author's calculations, using ETD data.

higher share of workers in agriculture and lower share of workers services that differentiate high- from low- and middle-income countries.

As we have already noted in Section 3, a limitation of ETD data is that it starts in 1990. What if we used GGDC data, where there is sectoral employment for many countries from the 1960s? We present our classification of countries in different stages of structural transformation using GGDC data in Table A2 in the Online Appendix (see Baymul and Sen 2019 for more details). Table A3 and Figures A1 to A4 present the sectoral employment share of countries over time from 1990 to 2010, both in the aggregate and by structural transformation group. Strikingly, the patterns of structural transformation we observed using ETD data are very similar to what we see when we use GGDC data which have a longer time span. This suggests that for developing countries, what is important in the analysis of structural transformation is not the period of analysis, but the structural characteristics of these countries that are broadly constant over time. In other words, very few countries that were structurally underdeveloped in the 1960s have been able to make the move to higher stages of structural transformation in the 2010s.[26] Clearly, this is an important point to keep in mind when studying patterns of structural transformation in the developing world.

So far our analysis has been based on averages across countries for the broad structural transformation groups, and for the entire ETD sample. How do agricultural, manufacturing, business services, and non-business services employment

---

[26] Of the countries that Baymul and Sen (2019) classified in different stages of structural trans-formation using GGDC data, only Senegal has moved from structurally underdeveloped to structurally developing and Brazil from structurally developing to structurally developed stages of structural transformation using the more recent ETD data.

shares evolve for individual countries over time? In the Online Appendix, we present line plots by countries of the movements in shares of agricultural employment, manufacturing employment, business services employment, and non-business services employment over the period 1990–2018, where we group the countries by stages of structural transformation. We start with the plots of agricultural employment share for structurally underdeveloped countries, structural developing countries, and structurally developed countries in Figures A5, A6, and A7 respectively.[27] For the structurally underdeveloped group, agricultural employment share remains at around 40–60 per cent by 2018. In some countries such as Burkina Faso, Bangladesh, Rwanda, and Vietnam, there is a rapid decrease in the share of workers in agriculture.[28] In other countries such as Mozambique, Uganda, and Tanzania, there is hardly any fall in agricultural employment share, suggesting that the rate of structural transformation is close to zero in these countries. For structurally developing countries, again, we see sharp declines in agricultural employment shares in some countries such as China and Senegal and near-stagnation in some other countries, such as Botswana, Lesotho, and Morocco.[29] For structurally developed countries, most workers are not employed in agriculture, by 2018.

We next look at the plots of manufacturing employment share for structurally underdeveloped countries, structural developing countries, and structurally developed countries in Figures A8, A9, and A10 respectively. Here, again, for structurally underdeveloped countries, we see a rapid rise in manufacturing employment share for countries such as Burkina Faso, Bangladesh, Kenya, and Vietnam, and very little change in manufacturing employment share for countries like Rwanda, Tanzania, and Zimbabwe. For structurally developing countries, countries such as Costa Rica, Turkey, and South Africa are already witnessing a fall in manufacturing employment share, while countries such as Sri Lanka, Lesotho, and Senegal are witnessing rapid increases in manufacturing employment share. For structurally developed countries, manufacturing employment share is either stable or falling in most of the countries in this group.

---

[27] Country codes used in the figures are provided in Online Appendix, Table A4.

[28] Of the countries in the structurally underdeveloped group, the countries most likely to make the transition to the structurally developing group in the next decade or less are Bangladesh, Nigeria, and Vietnam as in these countries, agricultural employment share is just one or two percentage points higher than services employment share and the rate of fall in agricultural employment share is fairly large. In all other countries, agricultural employment share is substantially larger than services employment share and/or the rate of decline in agricultural employment share is low.

[29] Of the countries in the structurally developing group, the country most likely to make the transition to the structurally developed group in the next decade or less is Turkey, where the share of employment in manufacturing is marginally less than the share of employment in agriculture. China and Costa Rica are also candidates for moving up to the next stage of structural transformation if they maintain their progress in moving workers out of agriculture.

We then look at the plots of business services employment share for structurally underdeveloped countries, structural developing countries, and structurally developed countries in Figures A11, A12, and A13 respectively. For the structurally underdeveloped countries, business services employment shares hardly show any increase, except in the case of Cambodia and Nigeria, and are at low levels. For the structurally developing group, there are several countries which show a sharp increase in business services employment share such as Colombia, Costa Rica, Turkey, and South Africa. For the structurally developed group, business services employment shares are at a high level and are mostly increasing for countries in this group.

Finally, we look at the plots of non-business services employment share for structurally underdeveloped countries, structural developing countries, and structurally developed countries in Figures A14, A15, and A16 respectively. For the structurally underdeveloped group, unlike in the case of business services, we see large increases in non-business services employment shares for most countries in this group. For the structurally developing countries, non-business services employment shares are high and are steadily increasing for most countries. For structurally developed countries, non-business services employment shares are also at high levels, but the rate of increase is not as high as for structurally underdeveloped and developing countries.

Overall, our country-level analysis substantiates what we have found at the aggregate level. While there is some heterogeneity in country experiences with structural transformation, several structurally underdeveloped countries have seen a slow decrease in agricultural employment shares, and the movement of workers, where it has occurred, has been mostly to non-business services and not to manufacturing and business services. In contrast, we see more dynamism in the structurally developing group of countries where there has been a fairly large increase in business services employment share. For structurally developed countries, both non-business and business services provide important sources of employment for their workers, along with manufacturing, in some cases.

Premature Deindustrialization?

As we have noted in Section 1, one important finding in the empirical literature on structural transformation is the inverted U-shaped nature of manufacturing employment share with respect to per capita income. As per capita income increases, manufacturing employment increases up to a certain level of per capita income. After this level, manufacturing employment share starts to decline. Rodrik (2016) has noted that the peak at which manufacturing employment share starts to decline is a lower level for low-income countries than what has

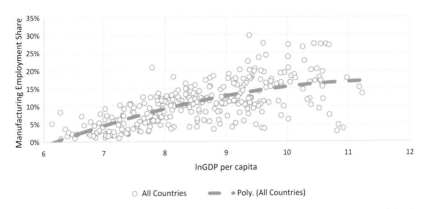

Figure 17 The relationship between manufacturing employment share and GDP per capita (US PPP dollars), all countries

Source: author's calculations, using ETD and the World Bank's *World Development Indicators* data

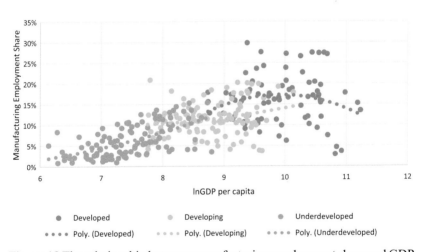

Figure 18 The relationship between manufacturing employment share and GDP per capita (US PPP dollars), by structural transformation group

Source: author's calculations, using ETD and the World Bank's *World Development Indicators* data.

been observed for the richer countries in the past. Furthermore, the peak of the manufacturing employment share is occurring at lower levels of income. Do we observe such a phenomenon of premature deindustrialization in the ETD data?

Figure 17 plots manufacturing employment share against GDP per capita for all the countries in the ETD data. Figure 18 provides a similar plot, now classifying the countries by the structural transformation group they belong to. As is evident from Figure 17, manufacturing employment share does start to level off as per capita income increases. Since we do not have most of the high-income countries in the ETD data, where manufacturing employment shares have been declining steadily since the 1980s, we are not able to observe the inverted U-shaped relationship between manufacturing employment share and per capita income (as Appendix Figure A.17 shows, this relationship is clear when we use GGDC data from 1960 to 2010, where the GGDC data also contain a larger number of high-income countries). When we look at the behaviour of manufacturing employment share with respect to per capita income by structural transformation group, we do not find clear evidence of premature deindustrialization (Figure 18). In fact, manufacturing employment shares do increase with per capita income for structurally underdeveloped countries (which are mostly the low-income countries). Kruse et al. (2021) also provide complementary evidence, also using ETD data, that also shows the absence of premature deindustrialization in low-income countries. They find that the manufacturing employment share has been increasing for many low-income countries in Asia and sub-Saharan Africa. They further find that several developing countries that had seen peak industrialization in the 1970s or 1980s, such as Ghana and Nigeria, are experiencing a manufacturing renaissance since the 2000s. As Figure 19 shows, the manufacturing employment share in sub-Saharan Africa and

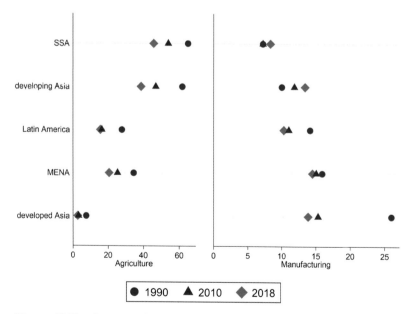

Figure 19 Employment shares in agriculture and manufacturing, by region

Notes: Employment shares in agriculture and manufacturing by region, unweighted averages; SSA: sub-Saharan Africa.

Source: Kruse, et al. (2021).

developing Asia has increased in the period 1990–2018, though in the case of sub-Saharan Africa, the increase has been fairly small.

What about the relationship between service employment share and per capita income? As before, we disaggregate services to business and non-business services. The relationship between business service employment share and per capita income for all countries and then by structural transformation group is presented in Figures 20 and 21 respectively. The relationship between non-business service employment share and per capita income for all countries and then by structural transformation group is presented in Figures 22 and 23 respectively. We find that there is no noticeable increase in business service employment share till a country reaches a certain level of income and then the increase in the share is fairly sharp, especially for structurally developed countries. We find the opposite phenomenon when it comes to non-business services, with the increase in the share of non-business services fairly rapid for structurally underdeveloped and developing groups of countries, and then levelling off for structurally developed countries. This suggests that as per capita income increases, the initial movement of workers from agriculture is to manufacturing and non-business services. However, as countries reach higher levels of income, there is a sizeable movement of workers to business services, with a relatively smaller proportion of workers moving to manufacturing and non-business services.

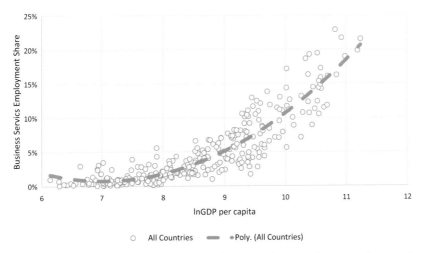

Figure 20 The relationship between business services employment share and GDP per capita (US PPP dollars), all countries

Source: author's calculations, using ETD and the World Bank's *World Development Indicators* data.

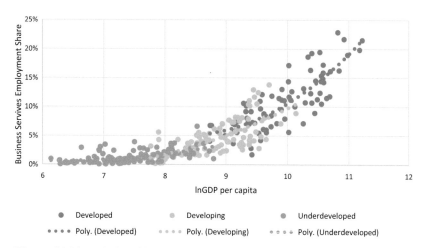

Figure 21 The relationship between business services employment share and GDP per capita (US PPP dollars), by structural transformation group

Source: author's calculations, using ETD and the World Bank's *World Development Indicators* data.

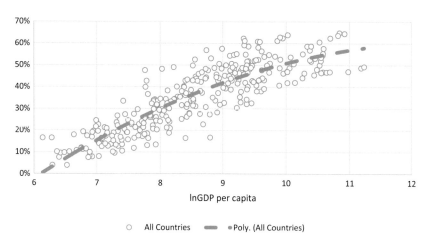

Figure 22 The relationship between non-business services employment share and GDP per capita (US PPP dollars), all countries

Source: author's calculations, using ETD and the World Bank's *World Development Indicators* data.

4.2 Patterns in Production Structure and Productivity

We now look at the patterns in sectoral real value added and labour productivity for all countries over time and by stage of structural transformation. With respect to real value added (where real value added is defined as gross

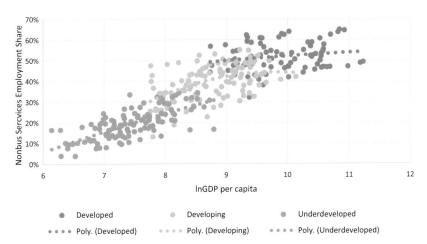

Figure 23 The relationship between non-business services employment share and GDP per capita (US PPP dollars), by structural transformation group

Source: author's calculations, using ETD and the World Bank's *World Development Indicators* data.

value added in 2015 local currency prices, millions), we find that the share of sectoral value added in agriculture has been falling steadily from 21 per cent in 1990–94 to 14 per cent in 2015–18 for all countries. The sectoral value added share in manufacturing industry and non-manufacturing industry is roughly constant at 16 per cent and 14 per cent, respectively, over time. The sectoral value added in services as a whole has increased from 49 per cent in 1990–94 to 55 per cent in 2015–18, with most of the services sub-sectors (Table 6) also showing an increase over time, barring the government and other sectors which has seen a decline in sectoral value added over time. Among the services sub-sectors, the largest absolute increase in terms of percentage points is in business services, from 5 per cent in 1990–94 to 9 per cent in 2015–18.

When looking at patterns in sectoral value added by stages of structural transformation, we see similar patterns for country groups that we observed for all countries (Table 7). The share of sectoral value added in agriculture has been falling steadily for structurally underdeveloped, structurally developing, and structurally developed countries over 1990–2018, and at the same time, there has been a sustained increase in the share of sectoral value added in business and non-business services for all country groups over time. The shares of sectoral value added in manufacturing industry and non-manufacturing industry have remained approximately the same for the

Table 6 Share of value added by stages of structural transformation over time, disaggregated sectors, all countries

Period	Agric.	Manufacturing Ind.	Non-manufacturing Ind.	Mining	Utilities	Construction	Services	Trade	Transport	Business	Financial	Govt. & Other
1990–94	21.1%	16.1%	14.3%	5.9%	2.5%	5.9%	48.5%	15.2%	5.2%	5.1%	4.1%	18.9%
1995–99	20.1%	16.4%	14.3%	5.7%	2.6%	5.9%	49.1%	15.6%	5.5%	5.5%	4.4%	18.2%
2000–04	18.9%	16.9%	14.1%	5.8%	2.7%	5.6%	50.1%	15.5%	5.7%	6.4%	4.3%	18.2%
2005–09	16.9%	16.9%	14.3%	5.8%	2.6%	5.8%	51.9%	16.3%	5.9%	7.4%	4.8%	17.5%
2010–14	15.3%	16.5%	14.2%	5.4%	2.5%	6.3%	54.0%	16.8%	5.9%	8.4%	5.3%	17.6%
2015–18	13.9%	16.2%	14.2%	4.9%	2.5%	6.7%	55.7%	17.0%	6.0%	9.0%	5.9%	17.9%

Notes: (a) Ind. Is Industry, Serv. Is Services, (b) Non-manufacturing industry is mining, utilities and construction; (c) Services is Trade, Transport, Business, Financial and Govt. and Other Services.

Source: author's calculations, from ETD.

Table 7 Share of value added by stages of structural transformation over time, by broad sectors and by country group

ST Group	Period	Agriculture	Manufacturing Ind.	Non-manufacturing Ind.	Business Services	Non-Business Services
Underdeveloped	1990–94	38%	10%	11%	7%	33%
Underdeveloped	1995–99	37%	11%	12%	7%	33%
Underdeveloped	2000–04	34%	11%	12%	8%	34%
Underdeveloped	2005–09	31%	12%	13%	9%	36%
Underdeveloped	2010–14	28%	12%	13%	10%	37%
Underdeveloped	2015–18	25%	12%	15%	11%	37%
Developing	1990–94	15%	19%	16%	8%	42%
Developing	1995–99	14%	19%	16%	9%	42%
Developing	2000–04	13%	20%	16%	10%	41%
Developing	2005–09	12%	19%	17%	11%	41%
Developing	2010–14	10%	18%	17%	13%	41%
Developing	2015–18	10%	18%	16%	14%	42%
Developed	1990–94	5.8%	20.5%	15.7%	14.2%	43.9%
Developed	1995–99	4.8%	20.5%	15.3%	15.1%	44.3%
Developed	2000–04	4.5%	20.7%	13.9%	16.5%	44.4%
Developed	2005–09	4.2%	20.9%	12.3%	18.4%	44.2%
Developed	2010–14	3.9%	20.6%	11.4%	20.0%	44.2%
Developed	2015–18	3.7%	19.9%	10.5%	21.6%	44.2%

Source: author's calculations, from ETD.

period 1990–2018. However, we also observe two clear differences in production structures across country groups. Firstly, with respect to the contribution of agriculture to value added, for structurally developed countries, it is a paltry 4 per cent. In contrast, for structurally underdeveloped and developing countries, the corresponding numbers are 25 and 10 per cent respectively. Secondly, the increase in the contribution of business services to total value added is far greater for structurally developed countries than for structurally underdeveloped and developing countries. By 2015–18, 22 per cent of value added for structurally developed countries was originating from business services, while the corresponding numbers for structurally underdeveloped and developing countries were 11 and 14 per cent respectively. In contrast, the differences in the contribution of non-business services to total value added are not particularly large by country group – 44 per cent of value added in structurally developed countries originated from non-business services in 2015–18. The corresponding numbers for structurally underdeveloped and developing countries were 37 and 42 per cent respectively. This suggests that the real difference in the patterns of structural transformation between structurally underdeveloped, developing, and developed countries is not in the growing importance of services per se (we do observe this is the case for all countries), but in the rise of the business services sector as major source of value added, the higher the country is in the stage of structural transformation.

Now turning to labour productivity (defined as real value added as a ratio of persons engaged), we find that for all countries, there has been no perceptible change in productivity for most sectors over time, except manufacturing industry where productivity roughly doubled over 1990–2018, and among services sub-sectors, trade and transportation also witnessed an increase (Table 8). In 2015–18, the most productive sectors were mining, utilities, and financial services, in that order. The most unproductive sectors were agriculture, the government, and other sectors and construction, with agriculture being the most unproductive sector by far.

Examining the evolution of labour productivity by stage of structural transformation over time, we find that there are striking productivity gaps across country groups in agriculture and manufacturing industry (Table 9). For example, by 2015–18, labour productivity in agriculture for structurally developed countries is around twenty-one times that of structurally underdeveloped countries and five times that of structurally developing countries. Similarly, for manufacturing industry, labour productivity for structurally developed countries is around twelve times that of structurally underdeveloped countries and five times that of structurally developing countries in the same period. For non-business services, labour

Table 8 Labour productivity, by disaggregated sectors over time, all countries

Period	Agric.	Manuf. Ind.	Non-manuf. Ind.	Mining	Utilities	Construction	Services	Trade	Transport	Business	Financial	Govt. & Other
1990–94	5	12	20	94	41	12	11	9	13	26	54	11
1995–99	5	14	21	110	49	12	12	10	14	24	48	11
2000–04	6	17	22	132	64	11	12	10	15	25	46	11
2005–09	7	19	22	122	68	12	14	11	18	24	47	12
2010–14	7	22	21	111	69	12	15	13	19	23	49	12
2015–18	7	23	21	111	72	13	16	14	20	23	55	13

Notes: (a) Ind. Is Industry, Serv. Is Services, (b) Non-manufacturing industry is mining, utilities, and construction; (c) Services is Trade, Transport, Business, Financial, and Govt. and Other Services.

Source: author's calculations, from ETD.

Table 9 Labour productivity by stages of structural transformation over time, by broad sectors and by country group

Country Group	Period	Agriculture	Manufacturing Ind.	Non-manufacturing Ind.	Business Services	Non-Business Services
Underdeveloped	1990–94	1	4	13	23	3
Underdeveloped	1995–99	1	4	12	18	3
Underdeveloped	2000–04	1	4	11	15	3
Underdeveloped	2005–09	1	4	11	14	3
Underdeveloped	2010–14	1	4	9	13	4
Underdeveloped	2015–18	1	5	9	14	4
Developing	1990–94	2	10	15	25	8
Developing	1995–99	2	11	16	24	8
Developing	2000–04	3	13	19	24	8
Developing	2005–09	3	15	22	25	9
Developing	2010–14	4	17	20	23	10
Developing	2015–18	4	17	19	25	11
Developed	1990–94	14	27	38	43	23
Developed	1995–99	15	35	40	44	25
Developed	2000–04	17	41	41	46	26
Developed	2005–09	19	48	40	49	29
Developed	2010–14	21	56	40	54	31
Developed	2015–18	21	60	40	59	32

Source: author's calculations, from ETD.

productivity in structurally developed countries is eight times that of structurally underdeveloped countries, and 1.5 times that of structurally developing countries. Interesting, the relative productivity gap between countries at different stages of structural transformation is the least in business services, with labour productivity in structurally developed countries being four times that of structurally underdeveloped countries, and 1.5 times that of structurally developing countries. This is because business services is by part the most productive sector, even for structurally underdeveloped countries, though it is not a sector which contributes many jobs.

Another interesting stylized fact of the evolution of productivity across countries in different stages of structural transformation and over time is that relative productivity gap between other sectors and agriculture (the least productive sector) narrows over time as countries reach higher stages of structural transformation. For example, for the most recent period, the ratio of productivity in manufacturing to productivity in agriculture is 5 for structurally underdeveloped countries, 4 for structurally developing countries, and 3 for structurally developed countries. This narrowing of relative productivity gaps across sectors at higher stages of structural transformation, along with the large and persistent within-sector productivity gaps across country groups, especially in the employment-intensive sectors, has clear implications for our understanding of the drivers of structural transformation. We will explore this issue in Section 5.

4.3 Trend Analysis

A key stylized fact that has been documented in the previous literature on structural transformation is that while workers initially move from agriculture to manufacturing at an early stage of structural transformation, leading to an increase in manufacturing employment share, over time, the share of manufacturing employment starts to fall after reaching a peak. This is because at more advanced stages of structural transformation, the movement of workers is to services from agriculture and manufacturing, with the services sector being the dominant sector in terms of employment at higher level of per capita income. We have already observed that this is the case in our analysis of patterns of sectoral employment in Section 4.3. We now examine this feature of structural transformation more systematically using trend analysis on the shares of sectoral employment.

To ascertain whether or not the shares of employment in manufacturing, business services, and non-business services follow a clear trend, we regress the share of employment in manufacturing on a time trend, averaging the data over five-year periods. We add the square of the time trend to account for the fact that the manufacturing employment share peaks at some point along a country's path of economic development. We do the same for business services and non-business services, except that here we do not add the square of a time trend as there is no clear turning point in these shares in the data. We first run the regressions for all economies, and then by country groups. We estimate these equations using random effects and report the results in Table 10.

For all economies, manufacturing employment share exhibits a decline over time – the coefficient on the time trend is negative and statistically significant (Col. (1)). However, there is no evidence of an inverse U-shaped behaviour with time, with the coefficient on the square of the time trend being statistically insignificant. Both business services and non-business services' share of total employment shows a clear increase over time for all economies (Cols. (2) and (3)). However, the trend analysis by country groups shows clear differences in the rate of change of the shares of employment in manufacturing, business services, and non-business services over time across the three economy groups.

As expected, manufacturing employment's share of structurally underdeveloped economies does not exhibit a clear inverted U-shaped behaviour over time – when both the time trend and its square are included in the regression, the former is insignificant (Col.(10)). When only the time trend is included, it is positive and statistically significant, suggesting that there is a movement into manufacturing for structurally underdeveloped economies over time (Col. (11)). We also obtain a similar finding for the shares of employment of business services and non-business services for structurally underdeveloped countries, with the coefficients on the time trends being positive and significant (Cols. (12) and (13)).

For structurally developing countries, the coefficient on the manufacturing employment share is statistically insignificant, indicating that there has been no clear movement of workers into manufacturing in 1990–2018 (Col. (7)). At the same time, there has been a movement of workers into business and non-business services, with the coefficients on the time trends positive and significant (Cols. (8) and (9)). For structurally developed countries, we observe the famous inverse U-shape in manufacturing employment share, with the coefficients on the time trend and the square of the time trend positive and negative, respectively, and both being statistically significant (Col. (4)). The movement of workers into business and non-business services is also clearly observed in the positive and significant coefficients in the time trends for these two employment shares (Cols. (5) and (6)).

One striking feature in the trends in employment shares across country groups is that the rate of increase in non-business services for structurally underdeveloped countries over time is higher than in the case of structurally developing and developed countries, as evident in the larger magnitude of the

Table 10 Trend analysis of employment shares

	All			ST Developed			
	Manuf. Emp.	**Bus. Serv. Emp.**	**Nonbus. Serv. Emp.**	**Manuf. Emp.**		**Bus. Serv. Emp.**	**Nonbus. Serv. Emp.**
	Col. (1)	Col. (2)	Col. (3)	Col. (4)	Col. (5)	Col. (6)	Col. (13)
Time trend	−0.693* (−1.73)	0.757*** (19.64)	2.039*** (20.87)	−2.733*** (−3.65)	–	1.300*** (17.77)	1.445 *** (10.39)
Square of time trend	0.078 (1.39)	–	–	0.177* (1.69)	–	–	–
Wald Chi-square	5.22*	385.91***	435.46***	98.37***	–	315.88***	107.86***
No. of countries	51	51	51	13	–	13	13
No. of observations	306	306	306	78	–	78	78
	Col. (7)	Col. (8)	Col. (9)	Col. (10)	Col. (11)	Col. (12)	Col. (13)

	ST Developing			ST Underdeveloped			
	Manuf. Emp.	**Bus. Serv. Emp.**	**Nonbus. Serv. Emp.**	**Manuf. Emp. (1)**	**Manuf. Emp. (2)**	**Bus. Serv. Emp.**	**Nonbus. Serv. Emp.**
Time trend	0.051 (0.11)	0.806*** (15.41)	2.025*** (10.57)	−0.041 (−0.10)	0.667*** (7.55)	0.337*** (8.69)	2.459*** (17.79)
Square of time trend	−0.013 (−0.20)	–	–	0.101* (1.69)	–	–	–
Wald Chi-square	0.22	237.61***	111.81***	61.62***	57.04***	75.53***	316.60***
No. of countries	19	19	19	19	19	19	19
No. of observations	114	114	114	114	114	114	114

Notes: *** indicates level of significance at the 1% level. T statistics in brackets. Employment shares as dependent variables range from 0 to 1.

Source: author's calculations based on ETD data.

coefficient on the time trend for non-business employment share for the structurally underdeveloped countries than the other two country groups. On the other hand, the rate of increase in business employment share is lower for structurally underdeveloped countries than that for structurally developed and underdeveloped economies, as evident by the differences in the magnitudes of coefficients on the respective time trends.

4.4 Concluding Remarks

To sum up, different paths of structural transformation are observed in the historical employment data for the fifty-one countries in the ETD database. Structurally developed countries have mostly followed the conventional path of structural transformation in which workers moved from agriculture to manufacturing and services first, and then out of manufacturing and into services. The inverse U-shaped nature of manufacturing employment share is less evident for structurally developing countries, though there has been a rapid increase in the movement of workers into business and non-business services. In contrast, manufacturing employment shares in structurally underdeveloped countries have shown a positive trend, with no signs as yet of these countries having reached the peak of manufacturing employment share as a group. However, what differentiates structurally underdeveloped countries from structurally developing and developed countries is the rate of change of employment in business versus non-business services: the movement of workers out of agriculture into non-business services has occurred at a more rapid pace than into business-services. Later in this Element, we will see why this difference in the movement of workers into business versus non-business services is important for understanding the long-term drivers of structural transformation and economic development.

5 Drivers of Structural Transformation

In Section 2, we provided an overview of the classical and neoclassical theoretical approaches to structural transformation. As we noted in our discussion of the classical and neoclassical approaches, much of the theoretical literature highlights two sets of factors that have been offered as the key drivers of structural transformation – differential productivity growth across sectors and changes in demand for sectoral output over time. In this section, we examine these two explanations in turn, using ETD. Further, we examine the explanatory power of a prototype neoclassical model of structural transformation – the Duarte-Restuccia model-that we discusss in greater detail in Appendix A1. Finally, we examine the role of globalization in influencing the pattern of structural transformation, taking inspiration from the recent theoretical developments which highlight the role of the open economy in understanding structural transformation.

5.1 The Role of Productivity Differentials across Sectors

Both the classical and neoclassical approaches to structural transformation highlight the role of relative productivity differentials across sectors in explaining why some countries do better than others in moving workers out of agriculture to manufacturing and services. According to these approaches, if productivity growth in agriculture outstrips productivity growth in manufacturing, leading to a fall in the relative demand for labour in agriculture, the share of workers in manufacturing will increase over time. A similar argument applies if productivity growth in agriculture outstrips productivity growth in services, which would lead to an increase in the share of workers in services over time. Put in another way, with higher agricultural productivity growth as compared to manufacturing productivity growth, there is a decline in manufacturing (services) productivity relative to that of agriculture (i.e., relative manufacturing productivity), and a shift of workers from agriculture to manufacturing (services).

To what extent can we attribute the patterns of structural transformation observed in Section 4 to differential productivity growth across sectors? To address this question, we first look at the behaviour of sectoral labour productivity for all economies and then by structural transformation country group. We then look at the relationship between changes in relative manufacturing productivity and changes in manufacturing employment share across countries and by structural transformation group. We follow this by looking at the relationship between changes in relative services productivity and changes in services employment share across countries and by structural transformation group. We also examine whether higher manufacturing productivity growth relative to services productivity growth is associated with shifts out of manufacturing to services.

Beginning with plots of sectoral labour productivity for all countries in ETD (Figure 24), we find that the ranking of sectoral productivity has not changed in the period 1990–2018, except manufacturing, which started out as having roughly the same level of productivity as non-business services and much lower than non-manufacturing productivity, but overtook the latter in the period 2005–2010. As expected, labour productivity in agriculture is the lowest, and labour productivity in non-business services the highest.

Next, examining the evolution of labour productivity for structurally underdeveloped countries, we find that, quite remarkably, manufacturing productivity is not very different than non-business services productivity, and far lower than business services and non-manufacturing industry productivities (Figure 25).

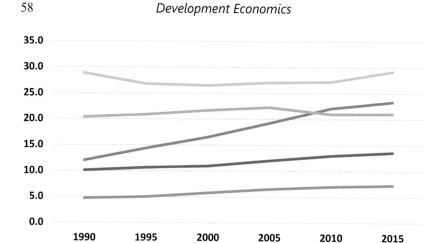

Figure 24 Sectoral labour productivity, all countries

Note: Agr: Agriculture, Manf: Manufacturing, Nonmanf: Non-manufacturing, Bus Serv: Business Services and Nonbus Serv: Non-business Services.

Source: author's calculations, from ETD.

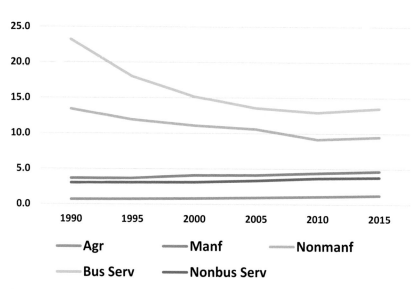

Figure 25 Sectoral labour productivity, structurally underdeveloped countries

Note: Agr: Agriculture, Manf: Manufacturing, Nonmanf: Non-manufacturing, Bus Serv: Business Services and Nonbus Serv: Non-business Services.

Source: author's calculations, from ETD.

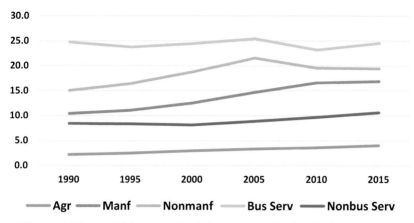

Figure 26 Sectoral labour productivity, structurally developing countries

Note: Agr: Agriculture, Manf: Manufacturing, Nonmanf: Non-manufacturing, Bus Serv: Business Services and Nonbus Serv: Non-business Services.

Source: author's calculations, from ETD.

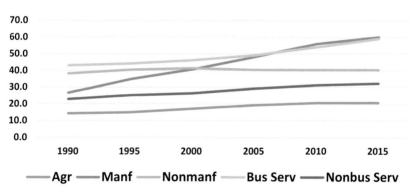

Figure 27 Sectoral labour productivity, structurally developed countries

Note: Agr: Agriculture, Manf: Manufacturing, Nonmanf: Non-manufacturing, Bus Serv: Business Services and Nonbus Serv: Non-business Services.

Source: author's calculations.

This is a surprising finding given that a large proportion of non-business services is neither tradable nor produced in competitive markets as in the case of manufacturing. With respect to structurally developing countries, we see that manufacturing productivity has been increasing over time and has almost caught up with non-manufacturing industry productivity (Figure 26). Finally, for structurally developed countries, productivity of manufacturing has increased sharply over time, and is very similar to business services productivity by 2018 (Figure 27).

From ETD we now look at the relationship between changes in relative manufacturing productivity and changes in manufacturing employment share, for all countries (Figure 28) and by structural transformation group (Figure 29). As expected, we see a negative relation between changes in relative manufacturing productivity and changes in manufacturing employment share for all countries. We also observe a similar relationship for structurally developing and underdeveloped countries. However, the relationship is much weaker for the structurally developed countries.

What about the relationship between changes in relative services productivity and changes in services employment share? We present the scatter plots for all countries in Figure 30 and by structural transformation group in Figure 31. As in the case of manufacturing, we see a negative relationship between changes in relative services productivity and changes in services employment share for all countries, and for structurally developing and underdeveloped countries, but the relationship is less evident in the case of structurally developed countries.

So far, our focus has been on differences in productivity growth of manufacturing/services relative to agriculture in explaining patterns of structural transformation. However, changes in sectoral productivity differentials between

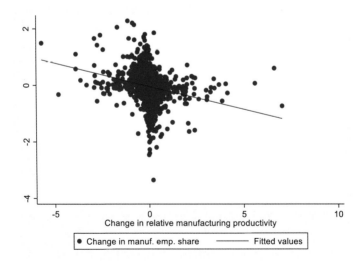

Figure 28 The relationship between change in relative manufacturing productivity and change in manufacturing employment share, all countries

Note: Relative Manufacturing Productivity=Manufacturing Labour Productivity/ Agricultural Labour Productivity.

Source: author's calculations, from ETD.

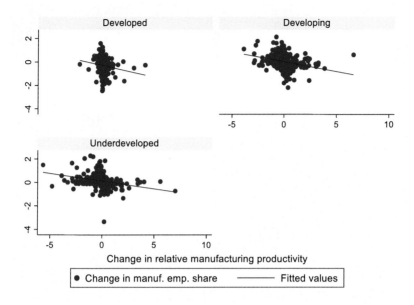

Figure 29 The relationship between change in relative manufacturing productivity and change in manufacturing employment share, by structural transformation group

Note: Relative Manufacturing Productivity=Manufacturing Labour Productivity/ Agricultural Labour Productivity.

Source: author's calculations, from ETD.

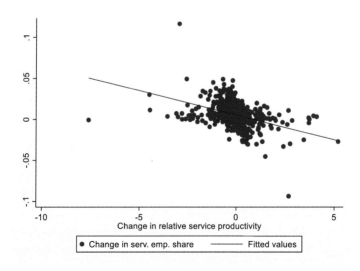

Figure 30 The relationship between change in relative services productivity and change in services employment share, all countries

Note: Relative Services Productivity=Services Labour Productivity/Agricultural Labour Productivity.

Source: author's calculations, from ETD.

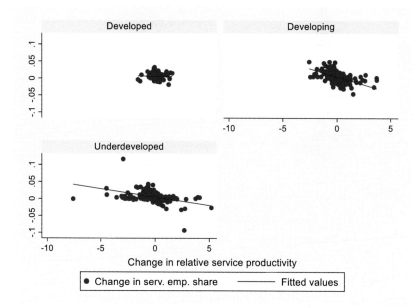

Figure 31 The relationship between change in relative services productivity and
change in services employment share, by structural transformation group

Note: Relative Services Productivity=Services Labour Productivity/Agricultural Labour
Productivity.

Source: author's calculations, from ETD.

manufacturing and services can also explain changes in manufacturing employment share, especially in contexts where a large proportion of the workforce is not employed in agriculture. In Figures 32 and 33, we look at the relationship between changes in the productivity differential between manufacturing and services and manufacturing employment share, for all countries and by structural transformation group respectively. Here, we observe a clear negative relationship between changes in the productivity differential between manufacturing and services and manufacturing employment share, both for all countries and for each of the structural transformation groups. The fact that we see the negative relationship between sectoral productivity differences and patterns of structural transformation for structurally developed countries in this case suggests that for these set of countries, the key sectoral productivity differential that matter for structural transformation is between manufacturing and services, and not between manufacturing and agriculture.

Overall, we find that the set of arguments that highlight the role of sectoral productivity differences in explaining structural transformation seems to find support in the data, at least in a descriptive sense. To examine this more

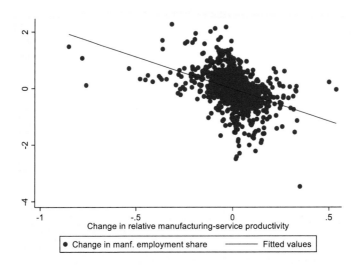

Figure 32 The relationship between change in the difference between
manufacturing and services productivity and change in manufacturing
employment share, all countries

Source: author's calculations, from ETD.

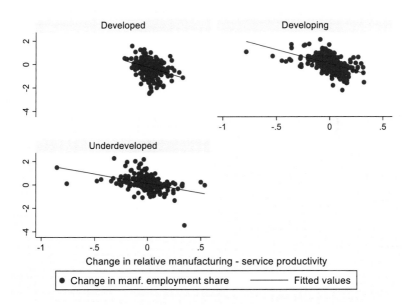

Figure 33 The relationship between change in the difference between
manufacturing and services productivity and change in manufacturing
employment share, by structural transformation group

Source: author's calculations, from ETD.

systematically, we run panel regressions of sectoral employment shares against sectoral relative productivity, with country fixed, for our ETD sample. To take into account the fact that business services productivity is substantially higher than non-services business services productivity, we disaggregate services employment into business services and non-business services employment and look at the role of business services productivity and non-services business services productivity separately. We present the results in Table 11. We find as expected that higher relative manufacturing productivity and relative services productivity are associated with lower manufacturing employment and services employment shares respectively. Interestingly, higher relative business services productivity is associated with higher business services employment share, suggesting that productivity increases in this sector may have a demand boosting effect. Therefore, there seems to be a reasonably strong argument for the productivity-based approach to structural transformation.[30]

Table 11 Regression results –productivity and structural transformation, all countries

Dependent Variable	Manufacturing Emp.	Business emp.	Non-business emp.
Method of Estimation	FE	FE	FE
Manufacturing Rel. Productivity	−0,391*** (0.124)	0.019 (0.067)	0.093 (0.188)
Business Serv Rel. Productivity	−0.043*** (0.014)	0.010* (0.005)	−0.023 (0.188)
Non-business Rel. Productivity	0.277 (0.236)	0.020 (0.126)	−1.183*** (0.188)
Number of observations	306	306	306
F statistic	5.87	16.96	44.78
Prob > F	0.00	0.00	0.00
R-squared (adjusted)	0.18	0.61	0.74

Note: FE is Fixed Effects, Emp. Is employment share; Rel. is relative.

Source: author's calculations using ETD data.

---

[30] We run the regressions by structural transformation group, with similar results.

5.2 The Role of Demand

What about the utility-based explanation of structural transformation? According to this explanation, if sectoral demand changes with increases in income, changes in income will lead to a re-allocation of resources towards sectors with higher income elasticities. Therefore, if there is a falling demand for agricultural goods and an increasing demand for services with increases in income, the utility-based explanation of structural transformation would argue that there will be movements of workers from agriculture to services as demand for services outputs increases relative to demand for agricultural outputs. To examine whether there is support for the demand-based theories of structural transformation, we plot Engel curves for key agricultural, manufacturing, and services outputs. We use the disaggregated data on sectoral household expenditures for our ETD countries that we obtain from the 2017 International Comparison Program (ICP). The ICP is a global statistical initiative to collect comparative price and expenditure data and estimate PPPs for the world's economies. The most recent data are available in the 2017 cycle, in which 176 countries participated. Economies participating in the ICP are required to provide a detailed breakdown of their national accounts expenditures for the reference year according to a common classification (World Bank 2017).The household consumption survey conducted as part of the ICP collects expenditure data for a wide range of goods and services for household consumption such as food, beverages, tobacco, clothing, footwear, utilities, furniture, household appliances, pharmaceuticals, private health care services, motor vehicles, transportation services, electronic equipment, communication services, catering services, accommodation services, recreational activities, personal hygiene, and other goods and services.

To construct sectoral Engel curves, we focus on food as the key expenditure item for agricultural goods, clothing and footwear as the key expenditure item for manufacturing and hotels and restaurant expenditures as the key expenditure item for services. We plot the Engel curves for food, clothing and footwear, and hotels and restaurants in Figures 34, 35, and 36 for all countries respectively. These curves show the relationship between the ratio of sectoral expenditures to GDP and per capita GDP, for food, clothing and footwear, and hotels and restaurants respectively. As is clear from Figure 34, the food Engel curve is negatively sloped, with food expenditures/GDP falling rapidly as per capita income increases. We also see a negatively sloped relationship between clothing and footwear expenditures as a ratio of income and GDP per capita, though the slope of the clothing and footwear Engel curve is not as steep as that for food (Figure 35). Finally, when we plot the Engel curve for hotels and restaurants expenditures as a ratio of GDP against per capita income, we find a positive

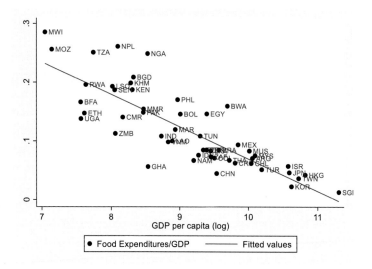

Figure 34 The Engel curve for food, all countries
Source: author's calculations, from ICP 2017.

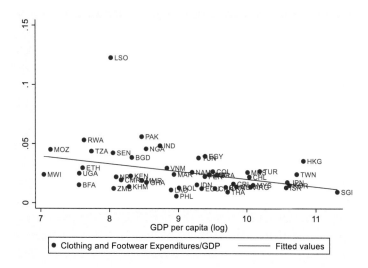

Figure 35 The Engel curve for clothing and footwear, all countries
Source: author's calculations, from ICP 2017.

relationship, suggesting that households spend more on hotel and restaurant services as their incomes increase (Figure 36). Overall, the descriptive evidence presented here supports the demand-based theories of structural

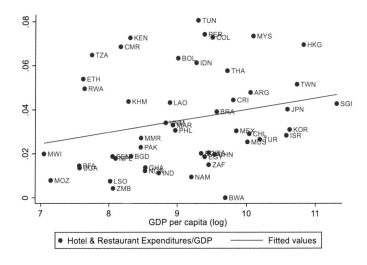

Figure 36 The Engel curve for hotels and restaurants, all countries
Source: author's calculations, from ICP 2017.

transformation – as incomes increase, there is a shift in demand from agriculture and manufacturing to services outputs, which is associated with a re-allocation of economic activity from agriculture and manufacturing (at a later stage of development for the latter) to services.

When we look at the sectoral Engel curves by structural transformation group (Figures 37–39), we find that the food Engel curve is downward-sloping for countries in all three stages of structural transformation. However, for the clothing and footwear Engel curve, the relationship is mostly negative for structurally developing countries, and flat for the structurally underdeveloped and developed group of countries. Similarly, for the hotels and restaurants Engel curve, the curve is positively sloped for structurally developing countries but mostly flat for structurally underdeveloped and developed group of countries. This suggests that while demand for agricultural output is falling at all stages of structural transformation, relative demand for services versus manufacturing seems to change most noticeably for structurally developing countries as compared to structurally underdeveloped and developed group of countries. Therefore, the demand-side explanation of structural transformation seems to find support from the data, again, at least in the descriptive sense.

Which of the two explanations – the supply-side and demand-side theories – have greater traction in explaining patterns of structural transformation, especially for low-income countries? As we noted in our discussion of the theories of structural transformation in Section 2, there is no clear consensus in the

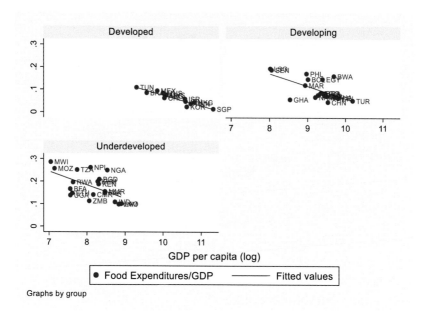

Figure 37 The Engel curve for food, by structural transformation group
Source: author's calculations, from ICP 2017.

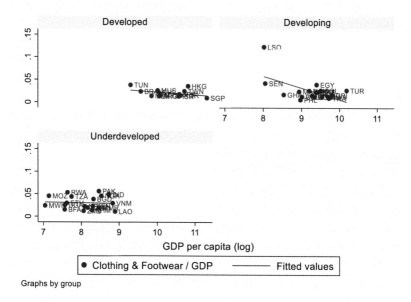

Figure 38 The Engel curve for clothing and footwear, by structural
transformation group
Source: author's calculations, from ICP 2017.

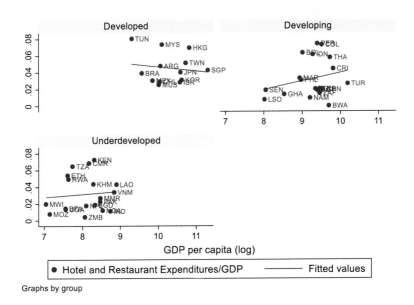

Graphs by group

Figure 39 The Engel Curve for Hotels and Restaurants, By Structural Transformation Group

Source: author's calculations, from ICP 2017.

literature on which set of factors – supply-side or demand-side – are more important, with both sets of factors finding empirical validity with the data. In principle, it is difficult to disentangle supply-side and demand-side factors from each other when examining the causes of structural transformation. As agricultural productivity growth takes place, workers are re-allocated to manufacturing and services. This leads to increases in income as manufacturing and services tend to be more productive than agriculture. As incomes rise, relative demand for goods that are inelastic in demand such as food falls (also known as Engel's law), leading to further re-allocation of workers away from agriculture. Thus, both supply-side and demand-side factors combine to determine the process of structural transformation.

The descriptive evidence that we have presented in this section provides some support for the argument that for structurally underdeveloped countries, one important reason why we see a slow movement of workers away from agriculture is that growth in agricultural productivity is weak (relative to growth in manufacturing and services productivity growth), as compared to countries in other stages of structural transformation (the large gap in agricultural productivity relative to non-agricultural productivity has also been observed by Gollin

Table 12 Simulation scenarios

Scenario	I	II	III	IV
Parameters	Baseline as in Duarte and Restuccia (2010); services = business services + non-business services	Baseline as in Duarte and Restuccia (2010); services = non-business services; manufacturing + business services as one sector	Using actual data for initial year and final year; services = business services + non-business services	Using actual data for initial year; services = non-business services; manufacturing + business services added together
a	0.01	0.01	Share of agricultural employment in 2018	Share of agricultural employment in 2018
$\bar{a}$	0.11	0.11	Share of agricultural employment in 1990	Share of agricultural employment in 1990
$\bar{s}$	0.89	0.89	Share of non-business and business services employment in 1990	Share of non-business services employment in 1990
b	0.04	0.04	Share of manufacturing employment during the period 1990–2018	Share of manufacturing + business services employment during the period 1990–2018
ρ	−1.5	−1.5	−1.5	−1.5

Source: author's illustration.

et al. 2014) . For these countries, which are mostly low-income, demand-side factors (which tend to kick in at higher levels of per capita income) may not as important as supply-side factors in explaining the rate of structural transformation. Demand-side factors (and especially the shift in relative demand away from food and manufacturing goods towards service expenditures) come into play more for structurally developing countries, as we observed from the sectoral Engel curves that we examined in this section. For structurally developed countries, along with demand-side factors, the crucial determinant of the rate of structural transformation is the rate of services productivity growth relative to the rate of manufacturing productivity growth. Therefore, while demand-side and supply-side factors are both important in explaining the patterns of structural transformation, their roles in determining the rate of structural transformation may differ, according to the stage of structural transformation a particular country may be in.

In Appendix A1, we describe a prototype neoclassical model of structural transformation (drawing from Duarte and Restuccia. 2010) which combines supply-side and demand-side explanations of structural transformation. We examine how well this model predicts current patterns of structural transformation for each country group under different scenarios described in Table 12 (see Appendix A1 for further details). Across all four scenarios, the model predicts actual employment

Table 13 How well does the Duarte-Restuccia model predict actual services and manufacturing employment shares?

	Service employment share – over- or under-prediction (percentage difference)				
	Scenarios				
Country Group	I	II	III	IV	Average
Underdeveloped	91	134	−93	−96	9
Developing	9	27	−82	−82	−32
Developed	−5	15	−34	−29	−13
	Manufacturing employment share – over- or under-prediction (percentage difference)				
	Scenarios				
Country Group	I	II	III	IV	Average
Underdeveloped	143	98	14	3	65
Developing	117	35	135	14	75
Developed	37	−25	118	−13	29

Note: Scenarios are as in Table 16. + is over-prediction and – is under-prediction.

Source: author's calculations, using ETD data.

shares in manufacturing and services in structurally developed countries well (see Table 13). However, there are systematic errors in prediction across all four scenarios for structurally developing and underdeveloping countries. This suggests that the prototype neoclassical model can provide a realistic explanation of structural transformation for richer countries but not for poor countries.

5.3 Globalization and Structural Transformation

The relationship between globalization and structural transformation remains contested in the literature. An earlier literature points to the benefits of outward orientation – with international trade, output and employment in the tradable sectors may increase through increased exports of tradable goods (Balassa 1982; Bhagwati 1988). Trade theoretic models suggest that the sectors which will expand through increased exports will be those sectors where the country in question has comparative advantage. In the model first proposed by Krueger (1977) and extended by Leamer (1987), the crucial variable determining trade and production structure is the land/labour ratio. Thus, land-abundant developing countries such as those in Africa and Latin America would be more likely to specialize in primary commodities, while developing countries in Asia would be more likely to specialize in (labour-intensive) manufactures. Wood (2003) finds persuasive evidence for the Krueger-Leamer variant of the Heckscher-Ohlin model – differences in factor endowments between Africa and Asia seem to explain why Africa's export structure is biased towards natural resource-based commodities rather than manufacturing exports. However, as Rodrik (2016) has pointed out, increased trade integration leading to imports displacing domestic manufacturing production may be responsible for the phenomenon of de-industrialization that is evident in many low-income countries, especially in sub-Saharan Africa. In addition, trade integration may lead to decreased labour intensity of manufacturing production (Sen 2019a). Therefore, whether increased trade integration facilitates a move of employment and production away from agriculture to manufacturing remains an empirical question, and depends on the factor endowments of the country in question and the nature of import competition.

While much of the earlier literature has focused on manufacturing as the key tradable sector capable of large-scale export expansion (since the demand for manufacturing goods is income elastic, while the demand for agricultural commodities is largely income inelastic), Baldwin and Forslid (2019) argue that with the recent globotics transformation, the export-oriented industrialization path followed by East Asian countries in the past may not be a realistic route to follow in the current environment. With the rapid adoption of digital technology in manufacturing processes, and the spread of the fourth industrial

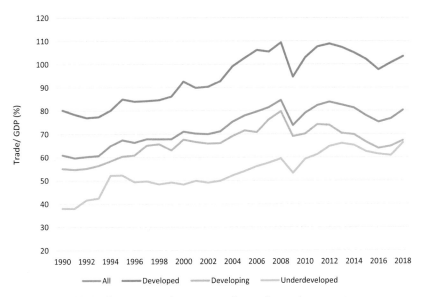

Figure 40 Trade openness by structural transformation country group

Source: author's calculations based on *World Development Indicators*.

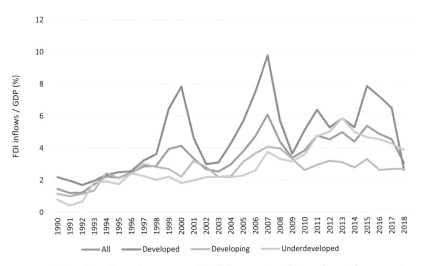

Figure 41 Foreign direct investment (FDI) by structural transformation country group

Source: author's calculations based on *World Development Indicators*.

revolution, many manufacturing tasks that could be undertaken by workers can now be performed by robots (UNIDO 2022). In contrast, with the decrease of service trade costs, developing countries may be able to increasingly export services, where they have a cost advantage as compared to developed countries

(Baldwin and Forslid 2019). This suggests that another route by which trade integration may affect the pattern of structural transformation in a developing country is by providing an opportunity for the services sector in the country to expand. This is a route that has been largely understudied in the extant literature.

While trade openness is conventionally seen as a reliable marker of globalization, foreign direct investment (FDI) is also an important mechanism for a developing country to obtain critical technologies from abroad as well as funds for investment when domestic investible resources are limited in supply (Dunning 1993). FDI is particularly important for participation in GVCs as it can remedy the scarcity of capital, technology, and management skills (World Bank 2020) as well as provide access to world markets (Brooks and Hill 2004). This suggests that FDI can also play an important role in influencing the rate of structural transformation as it can facilitate the movement of workers away from agriculture to basic labour-intensive manufacturing activities (such as clothing and footwear) at first, and then on to technology-intensive manufacturing activities such as electronics and automobile production and services such as IT and finance (Anzolin et al. 2022).

How do the patterns of trade openness (defined as exports+imports/GDP) and FDI (as a ratio of GDP) differ across our structural transformation country groups? In Figure 40, we plot the levels of trade-openness for all fifty-one countries and by structural transformation group. As is clear from the figure, while trade-openness is increasing across all country groups, trade openness levels are consistently higher for structurally developed countries, followed by structurally developing countries, and then followed by structurally underdeveloped countries. We see a similar pattern for FDI as a share of GDP, though there is more volatility in FDI as compared to trade openness, year by year (Figure 41). Interestingly, FDI in structurally developed and developing countries fell to levels in structurally underdeveloped countries in the last year of our period of analysis (2018).

We now examine whether increased levels of trade openness and FDI is associated with increased employment shares of manufacturing, business services, and non-business services using regression analysis. We run panel regressions of employment shares of manufacturing, business services, and non-business services on trade openness (defined as exports+imports/GDP) and foreign direct investment (as a ratio of GDP). We do this for all countries in ETD and then by structural transformation group. We use country fixed effects in all our regressions to take into account unobserved country-specific characteristics (such as factor endowments) that may be associated with both increased openness and attractiveness to FDI and rates of structural transformation.

With respect to the control variables, we use three basic controls – per capita income, human capital, and government consumption (to capture the size of the government sector). Per capita income functions as an omnibus control, and takes into account a feature that we have already observed earlier in this Element – that manufacturing employment shares peak at a certain level of economic development. Human capital is likely to play a complementary role to FDI in sectors such as manufacturing and business services (Blomström and Kokko 2002). Finally, there may be a positive association between the size of the government and trade openness as a large public sector may be used as a mechanism to provide social insurance against external risk (Rodrik 1998).

We present the results in Table 14 and Table 15. For all countries, we see that FDI has a negative and statistically significant effect on manufacturing employment share, but the coefficient on FDI is statistically insignificant for the regressions on business services and non-business services employment shares (Table 14). Trade has no discernible effect on the employment shares of manufacturing, business services, and non-business services. For structurally developed countries, trade and FDI have positive and negative statistically significant effects on manufacturing employment share. Interestingly, FDI has a positive and statistically significant effect on business services and non-business services employment shares for structurally developed countries (Table 14). For structurally developing countries, trade and FDI have no discernible effects on any of the three employment shares (Table 15). However, for structurally underdeveloped countries, trade has a positive and statistically significant effect on manufacturing employment share, while FDI has a negative and statistically significant effect on manufacturing employment share. There are no discernible effects on any of the other two employment shares (Table 15).

5.4 Concluding Remarks

In this section, we assess the relevance of the two sets of key factors that have been offered to explain patterns of structural transformation. One set is the role of productivity differentials across sectors, and the second is the role of demand-side factors as captured by sectoral Engel curves. We find that both these explanations have empirical support, using the ETD data as well as other complementary data sets. This suggests that our understanding of structural transformation must take into account the fact that both supply-side and demand-side factors play a role in explaining the movement of workers from agriculture to manufacturing and services. This underscores a basic insight that we obtain from economists such as Hollis Chenery, Moses Syrquin, and Simon Kuznets – that structural transformation is a complex phenomenon with the contribution of multiple factors. Therefore, it is not possible to isolate the primacy of one factor over another in our understanding of structural transformation. This is reinforced by the fact that a prototype model of structural

Table 14 The correlates of structural transformation, all and structurally developed countries

Dependent Var:	Manuf.	Business Services	Non-business Services	Manuf.	Business Services	Non-business Services
Country Group:	All	All	All	Developed	Developed	Developed
Trade	0.023	0.003	0.006	0.042**	0.004	−0.037
	(0.019)	(0.007)	(0.017)	(0.014)	(0.007)	(0.022)
FDI	−0.300**	0.058	−0.019	−0.575***	0.112**	0.191*
	(0.143)	(0.063)	(0.069)	(0.075)	(0.046)	(0.095)
Government Consumption	−0.149***	0.049*	−0.056	−0.060	−0.004	0.069
	(0.046)	(0.025)	(0.065)	(0.075)	(0.043)	(0.109)
Human Capital	−5.578***	2.380**	−3.814*	4.112**	0.246	−2.980
	(1.532)	(0.983)	(2.251)	(1.891)	(1.356)	(3.084)
Ln GDP per capita	1.400	−0.834	0.825	−0.149	−1.500	−2.879
	(1.034)	(0.594)	(1.894)	(1.570)	(1.080)	(2.331)
Number of observations	297	297	297	78	78	78
F statistic	4.76	14.40	23.18	228.93	337.53	27.82
Prob > F	0.00	0.00	0.00	0.00	0.00	0.00
R-squared	0.238308	0.6507	0.696453	0.816047	0.873785	0.719181

Note: Dependent variables are shares in total employment; *, ** and *** significant at 10, 5 and 1 per cent level respectively; Trade is Exports + Imports as a ratio of GDP (data are taken from the World Development Indicators); FDI is Inward FDI as a ratio of GDP (data are taken from the World Development Indicators); Government consumption is the share of government consumption at current PPPs (data from Penn World Table (PWT) 11.0; Human capital index, based on years of schooling and returns to education is taken from the PWT 11.0: Ln GDP per capita is the natural logarithmic values of output-side Gross Domestic Product (GDP) per capita at chained PPPs US dollars in 2017 (data taken from PWT 11.0).

Source: author's calculations.

Table 15 The correlates of structural transformation, structurally underdeveloped and developing countries

Dependent Var:	Manuf-	Business Services	Non-business Services	Manuf.	Business Services	Non-business Services
Country Group:	Developing	Developing	Developing	Underdeveloped	Underdeveloped	Underdeveloped
Trade	−0.005	0.000	0.033	0.058***	−0.006	0.012
	(0.027)	(0.014)	(0.036)	(0.019)	(0.010)	(0.037)
FDI	−0.055	−0.003	0.453	−0.166**	0.018	−0.069
	(0.130)	(0.076)	(0.340)	(0.064)	(0.033)	(0.140)
Government Consumption	−0.117	0.034	−0.255*	−0.054	−0.011	0.052
	(0.085)	(0.042)	(0.133)	(0.058)	(0.027)	(0.107)
Human Capital	−1.857	−0.527	−0.981	−2.542	0.942	3.182
	(2.040)	(1.979)	(4.317)	(3.797)	(1.299)	(7.802)
Ln GDP per capita	0.149	−0.987	−3.023	−1.743*	1.033**	−0.459
	(2.431)	(1.013)	(4.134)	(0.963)	(0.466)	(2.596)
Number of observations	111	111	111	108	108	108
F statistic	1.99	13.48	12.97	8.95	20.55	12.32
Prob > F	0.101898	0.00	0.00	0.00	0.00	0.00
R-squared	0.024439	0.705249	0.731884	0.48753	0.492342	0.753572

Note: Dependent variables are shares in total employment; *, ** and *** significant at 10, 5 and 1 per cent level respectively; Trade is Exports + Imports as a ratio of GDP (data are taken from the World Development Indicators); FDI is Inward FDI as a ratio of GDP (data are taken from the World Development Indicators); Government consumption is the share of government consumption at current PPPs (data from Penn World Table (PWT) 11.0; Human capital index, based on years of schooling and returns to education is taken from the PWT 11.0: Ln GDP per capita is the natural logarithmic values of output-side Gross Domestic Product (GDP) per capita at chained PPPs US dollars in 2017 (data taken from PWT 11.0).

Source: author's calculations.

transformation does well in explaining the pattern of structural transformation in developed economies but not so for developing economies, especially in the low-income world (see Annexe A1).

Our finding that trade has a positive effect on manufacturing employment share for structurally underdeveloped group seems to go against the argument by Rodrik (2016) that globalization has contributed to de-industrialization in low-income countries. On the other hand, our finding on the negative effect of FDI on manufacturing employment share for all countries and for the structurally developed and underdeveloped group seems to suggest that the technology that is incorporated in FDI may be labour-displacing and may not contribute to the movement of workers from agriculture to manufacturing. FDI does seem to have a positive effect on business and non-business services employment shares, but this seems to only hold for structurally developed countries. Overall, our findings on the role of globalization in influencing the pattern of structural transformation suggest a nuanced picture, with the relationship between globalization and structural transformation depending on whether the measure of globalization is trade openness or FDI, whether the sector in consideration is manufacturing or services, and whether the country is structurally developed, developing, or underdeveloped.

6 The Kuznets Process: Structural Transformation and Inequality

What are the implications of consequences of structural transformation for economic development? Does structural transformation exacerbate inequality, and if so, how? In this section, we will examine the consequences of structural transformation, focusing on inequality.[31]

As noted in Section 1, one of the most well-known findings in the literature on structural transformation is the inverted U-shaped relationship between structural transformation and inequality. As pointed out by Kuznets (1955), in the early process of structural transformation, inequality increases as workers move from a sector with low average incomes and lower within-sector inequality – agriculture – to sectors with higher average income and higher within-sector inequality, such as manufacturing and services. However, at higher stages of structural transformation, as incomes increase, countries are more likely to enact redistributive policies, leading to a decrease in inequality – the so-called Kuznets process (Anand and Kanbur 1993b). In this section, we examine the relationship between structural transformation and inequality, for all countries and by stage of structural

---

[31] This section draws from Baymul and Sen (2020). The analysis in the Baymul-Sen paper has been updated in this section using ETD data.

transformation. In examining the impact of structural transformation on inequality, we differentiate between manufacturing-driven structural transformation and services-driven structural transformation. As we will argue in this section, the implications of manufacturing-driven structural transformation on inequality may be quite different than that of services-driven structural transformation. Our examination of the relationship between structural transformation and inequality uses both descriptive and econometric methods.

We first begin with an exposition of the Kuznets process. We then present some stylized facts about structural transformation, inequality, and poverty. We then discuss the methodology used in the econometric analysis. We next discuss the results of the econometric analysis. We end with some concluding remarks.

6.1 The Kuznets Process

In his classic 1955 paper, Kuznets suggested that in the early phase of economic development, inequality will increase. At a later phase of economic development, as governments follow redistributive policies combining progressive taxation with welfare spending, inequality may decrease. The core of Kuznets's argument on the relationship between inequality and development is captured in the following paragraph extracted from his 1955 paper:

> An invariable accompaniment of growth in developed countries is the shift away from agriculture, a process usually referred to as industrialization and urbanization. The income distribution of total population in the simplest model, may therefore be viewed as a combination of the total income distributions of the rural and urban populations. What little we know of the structure of the two component income distributions reveals that a) the average per capita income of the rural population is usually lower than that of the urban; b) inequality in the percentage shares within the distribution for the rural population is somewhat narrower than that in the urban population ... Operating with this simple model, what conclusions do we reach? First, all other conditions being equal, the increasing weight of the urban population means an increasing share for the more unequal of the two component distributions. Second, the relative difference in per capita income between the rural and urban populations does not necessarily shift downward in the process of economic growth; indeed, there is some evidence to suggest that it is stable at best, and tends to widen because per capita productivity in urban pursuits increases more rapidly than in agriculture. If this is so, inequality in total income distribution should increase. (pp. 7–8)

The Kuznets process of widening inequality with structural transformation (i.e., movement of workers away from agriculture) can be described as composed of two sub-processes: (i) between-sector inequality: a movement of the population from a sector characterized **by lower mean income** to a sector characterized by **higher mean income**, and (ii) within-sector inequality: the movement of the population from a sector with **low within-sector inequality** to a sector with **higher within-sector inequality**. If both sub-processes work in the same direction – that is, if the movement of workers is from a sector with both a low mean and a low variance in incomes to a sector with a higher mean and high variance in incomes, then structural transformation will unambiguously increase inequality. However, if the movement of workers is from a sector with low mean income but higher variance of income to a sector with a higher mean income but lower variance in income, then it is less obvious that inequality will necessarily increase.

Following Anand and Kanbur (1993a), we provide a diagrammatic exposition of the Kuznets process to make clear the contribution of between-sector (or group) inequality and within-sector (or group) inequality to overall inequality.[32] Let I be the overall measure of inequality in a given country and let x be the share of workers in the non-agricultural sector. For the sake of exposition, let us assume that there is only one non-agricultural sector, so that we do not make a distinction between the manufacturing and services sectors. Let the working population of the country be normalized to one. Define between-sector (or group) inequality as the inequality in the income distribution when a fraction x of the working population receives income u_1 and the remaining fraction, 1-x, receives income u_2 (where between-group inequality is defined as the value of the inequality measure when everyone in the sector receives the mean income of the sector). Following Kuznets, we can assume that the mean income of the non-agricultural sector is higher than that of the agricultural sector – that is, $u_1 > u_2$.

It is clear from between-group inequality must be zero at both x=0 and x=1, and must be positive elsewhere – that is, when all workers are either in the agricultural sector or in the non-agricultural sector, there can be no between-group inequality. However, in the range where x is higher than 0 but less than 1, inequality will first increase with increasing x, then fall (as captured in Figure 42). This is because with low x, there are more workers in the low-income sector (in our example, agriculture) than in the high-income sector, so that between-sector income differences are considerable. However, once a larger proportion of workers are in the high-income sector, between-group inequality starts falling, till it reaches zero when all workers are in the high-income sector.

---

[32] This exposition depends on the assumption that the inequality measures we are considering are decomposable. Among the inequality measures available in the literature, the variance of log income and mean log deviation (which is Theil's second index) has such decomposition properties – see Robinson (1976) and Kanbur (2017).

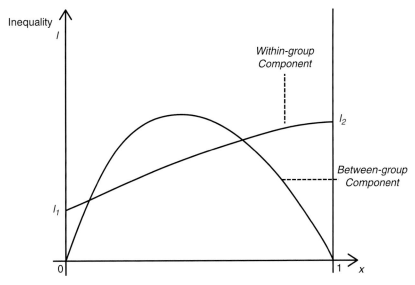

Figure 42 The Kuznets process

Source: adapted from Anand and Kanbur (1993a).

Now consider the behaviour of within-group inequality. Defining within-group inequality as the difference between overall inequality and between-group inequality, its movement with the increase in x will depend on the assumptions that one makes on within-group inequality in the non-agricultural sector versus the agricultural sector. If one assumes that there is higher within-group inequality in the non-agricultural sector than in the agricultural sector (as seems to be implied by Kuznets), then the within-group inequality component of overall inequality will strictly increase as x increases – that is, within-group inequality will increase with structural transformation (as shown in Figure 42).

The combination of the behaviour of between-group inequality and within-group inequality may lead to the well-known inverted relationship between structural transformation and inequality – in Figure 42, as x increases, there is an unambiguous increase in inequality; however, once a certain x is reached, if the between-group component dominates the within-group component, inequality will start declining.

The Kuznets process as described above does not differentiate between whether the movement of workers from agriculture is to manufacturing or services. Would the effects of manufacturing-driven structural transformation be different than that for services-driven structural transformation? There are several reasons to expect why the relationship may be different for manufacturing-driven structural transformation than for services-driven structural transformation. Firstly, manufacturing may have lower within-sector inequality in the initial stages of industrialization than services, if most of the increase in manufacturing employment is in labour-intensive activities such as garments and footwear. Secondly, manufacturing activity tends to be factory-based and in the formal sector (in contrast to the services sector, where a large part of economic activity is in the informal sector), where labour markets are characterized by minimum wages and other labour regulations. This is likely to lead to wage compression and, therefore, relatively low within-sector inequality. In contrast, a large of part of the employment created in the services may be self-employment in the poorly paid informal sector (such as household enterprises in the trade, hotels and restaurants sector), which may exist with well-paid jobs in the formal services sector (such as banking and finance), leading to higher within-sector inequality. For these reasons, we look at the effect of manufacturing employment share on inequality separately from that of services employment share.

6.2 The Relationship between Structural Transformation, Inequality and Poverty

Data for income inequality are taken from the newly launched WIID Companion (see Gradin 2021). WIID Companion provides standardized income inequality measures drawn from World Income Inequality Database (WIID) of the United Nations University – World Institute for Development Economics Research (UNU-WIDER).[33] This data set has been used extensively in the literature (see Ackland et al. 2013; Roope et al. 2018), and is widely regarded as the most reliable data on inequality for developing (and developed) countries. We use Net Ginis, which measure net per capita income inequality in a country in a given year.

We first look at the overall relationship between manufacturing employment share and inequality, then by stage of structural transformation. In the overall sample, we see a clear negative relationship between manufacturing-driven structural transformation and inequality (Figure 43). By stage of transformation, the negative relationship between manufacturing employment share and inequality is particularly evident for structurally developing countries (Figure 44). The relationship is weaker for structurally underdeveloped countries. For structurally developed countries, we see an inverted U-shaped relationship.

We next look at the relationship between services employment share and inequality, for the overall sample and then by stage of structural transformation. We do not see a clear relationship in the overall sample (Figure 45). By stage of structural transformation, we see a positive relationship for structurally

---

[33] WIID Companion contains information for 196 countries and four historical entities, with at least one year observation between 1940 and 2019 (except for Japan which starts in 1890).

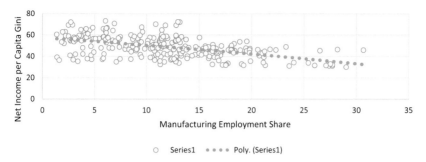

Figure 43 The relationship between manufacturing employment share and inequality, all countries

Source: author's calculations, from ETD and WIID Companion.

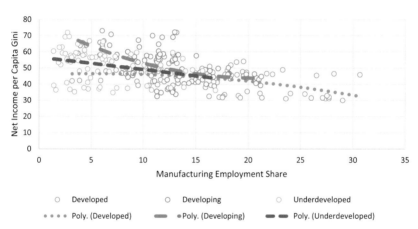

Figure 44 The relationship between manufacturing employment share and inequality, by stage of structural transformation

Source: author's calculations, from ETD and WIID Companion.

developing and no clear relationship for structurally underdeveloped and developed countries (Figure 46). Overall, the scatter plots suggests that there is a negative relationship between manufacturing-driven structural transformation and inequality and a lack of a clear relationship between services-driven structural transformation and inequality.

We supplement our descriptive analysis of the relationship between structural transformation and inequality by also looking at the relationship between structural transformation and poverty, where the latter is the poverty headcount ratio measured using the USD1.90 a day poverty line

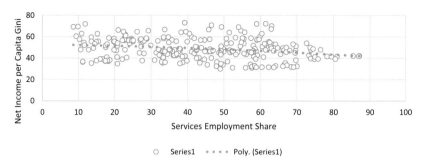

Figure 45 The relationship between services employment share and inequality,
all countries

Source: author's calculations, from ETD and WIID Companion.

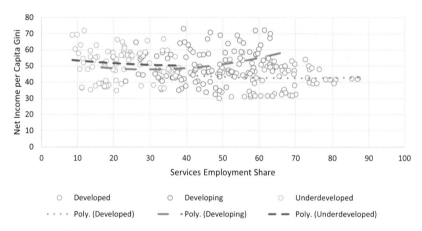

Figure 46 The relationship between services employment share and inequality,
by stage of structural transformation

Source: author's calculations, from ETD and WIID Companion.

(in Purchasing Power Parity terms). We do this first for manufacturing in
Figures 47 and 48, and then for services in Figures 49 and 50. We find that there
is a strong negative relationship between manufacturing employment share and
headcount poverty – as workers move into manufacturing, poverty declines
(Figure 47). The negative relationship is more evident for structurally underdeveloped countries; less so for structurally developing and developed countries
(Figure 48). Similarly, we see a negative relationship between services employment share and poverty for all countries (Figure 49). This negative relationship
is evident for countries in all three stages of structural transformation

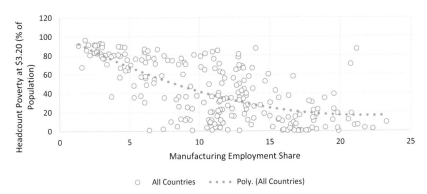

Figure 47 The relationship between manufacturing employment share and poverty, all countries

Source: author's calculations, from ETD and *World Development Indicators*.

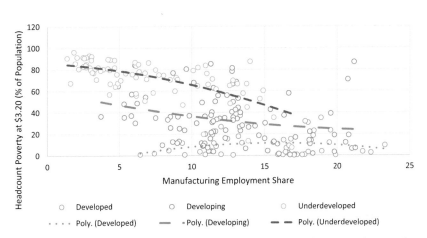

Figure 48 The relationship between manufacturing employment share and poverty, by stage of structural transformation

Source: author's calculations, from ETD and *World Development Indicators*.

(Figure 50). Clearly, both manufacturing-driven and services-driven structural transformation is associated with lower poverty. Both sectors have higher productivity than agriculture, and as workers obtain higher-paid jobs in sectors other than agriculture, poverty in the country starts to decline.

We now proceed to an econometric analysis of the relationship between structural transformation and inequality. We next discuss the econometric methodology that we will use in the analysis.

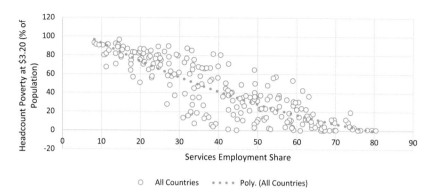

Figure 49 The relationship between services employment share and poverty, all countries

Source: author's calculations, from ETD and *World Development Indicators*.

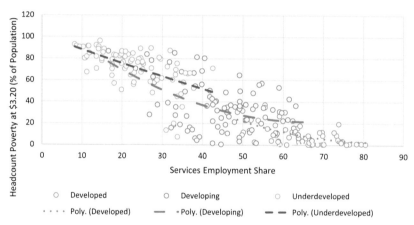

Figure 50 The relationship between services employment share and poverty, by stage of structural transformation

Source: author's calculations, from ETD and *World Development Indicators*.

6.3 Methodology

We are interested in the two following questions: (a) what are the effects of manufacturing-driven structural transformation on income inequality, and do the effects differ by the path of structural transformation a country is in, and (b) what are the effects of services-driven structural transformation on income inequality, and how are they different from the effects of manufacturing-driven structural transformation? To address these questions, we estimate the marginal impact of an increase in the shares of

employment in manufacturing and services on inequality with the following equation:

$$Gini_{it} = \beta_1 Manufacturing_{it} + \beta_2 Manufacturing_{it}^2$$
$$+ \beta_3 Nonmanufacturing_{it} + \beta_4 Services_{it} + \beta_5 Services_{it}^2$$
$$+ \beta_X X_{it} + \sigma_t + a_i + u_{it} \qquad \text{Equation (6.1)}$$

where i denotes country, and t denotes period. Manufacturing, Non-manufacturing
and Services are the employment shares of country i in period t in these sectors.[34]
Since we are interested in the marginal impact of manufacturing employment
share on inequality, we control for the employment shares of the other sectors. X is
a vector of other controls, which we discuss below, and σ_t and a_i are period and
country dummies.[35]

In Equation (6.1), we allow a non-linear effect of manufacturing and services
employment shares on inequality – as suggested by the Kuznets postulate that
inequality may first increase, then decrease with structural transformation (such
a quadratic relationship between employment share and inequality would not be
expected for non-manufacturing).

We estimate Equation (6.1) first for all countries, then for countries in
different stages of structural transformation.

As we noted in Section 3, the ETD database does not include many
high-income countries. Given the lack of inclusion of countries which have
reached the most mature stage of structural transformation in ETD, there
may be sample selection bias if we confine our analysis to low- and
middle-income countries (with two high-income countries – Korea and
Japan). For this reason, we also estimated Equation (6.1) using the ETD
database, and then by combining the countries that are there in the GGDC
data and not in ETD with the ETD database (for the period 1990–2010).
While we do not report the results here due to constraints of space, our
findings using the combined ETD-GGDC database were identical to what
we obtained when we used the ETD database.

We use a parsimonious sector of controls – these are per capita income, human
capital, trade, and government consumption (to capture the size of the government sector). Per capita income may have an independent effect on inequality (by
providing more resources for redistribution) over and above through the effect of
structural transformation on the level of economic development. Countries with

---

[34] Non-manufacturing comprises utilities, construction, and mining.
[35] Since the Gini coefficient is bounded by zero from below and 1 from the top, one concern would
be that Least Squares may not be an appropriate econometric strategy, given that the dependent
variable is censored. However, in our case, most values of the Gini lie between 0.3 and 0.8, with
very few observations approaching zero or 1.

higher levels of human capital are likely to see lower inequality as a higher supply of human capital would lead to lower wage inequality (Castello-Climent and Doménech 2014). At the same time, a larger supply of more educated workers may lead to the growth of more sophisticated service sector activities (such as business services), which may increase inequality. Trade may lower inequality by increasing the demand and wages for abundant low-skilled workers (Goldberg and Pavnik 2007). On the other hand, trade can increase inequality via trade-induced technological progress that is biased towards skilled labour and capital (Wood 1994; Feenstra and Hanson 2003). Finally, the larger the size of the government, the lower may be inequality (Dabla-Norris et al. 2015).[36]

We estimate Equation (6.1) by panel fixed effects regressions to control for time-invariant country characteristics (such as the country's factor endowments) that may explain both the pattern of structural transformation and inequality.[37] We also include time dummies to control for common global shocks that may affect structural transformation and inequality.[38] We use five-year period averaged data as we do not have annual observations on the Gini for many low-income countries, with 2015–18 data averaged over three years.[39] We have 258 observations for the 51 countries for the period 1990–2018.

6.4 Results

We present the results of the set of panel regressions that aim to investigate the relationship between the manufacturing and services employment shares and income inequality using ETD in Table 16.

We begin with a discussion of the effect of an increase in the shares of employment in manufacturing and services on inequality for all countries (Col. (I)). We do not find any evidence that increases in manufacturing and services employment share have a discernible effect on inequality – the coefficients on manufacturing and services employment shares and their squares are statistically insignificant. We then estimate Equation (1) by country group at different stages of structural transformation in Cols. (II) to (IV). For structurally underdeveloped countries, manufacturing employment share does not have any effect on inequality, but there is an U-shaped relationship

---

[36] The data on human capital and government consumption are taken from the Penn World Table 10.0, while the data on trade are taken from the World Bank's *World Development Indicators*.

[37] For example, countries with more favourable endowments of unskilled labour may have both larger manufacturing sectors and lower inequality (see Wood 2017).

[38] For example, a boom in global commodity prices may lead to a rise in employment in primary commodity sectors coinciding with an increase in inequality as incomes increase in high-rent, natural resource–intensive activities.

[39] We also estimated Equation (6.1) using annual data, with no change in our results.

Table 16 Regression results

	I All	II Underdeveloped	III Developing	IV Developed	All
Manufacturing	0.39 (0.45)	0.10 (1.30)	0.19 (1.20)	1.32** (0.66)	−1.06** (0.45)
Manufacturing^2	−0.02 (0.01)	−0.03 (0.06)	−0.02 (0.04)	−0.06*** (0.02)	0.01* (0.008)
Non-manufacturing	−0.29 (0.27)	−0.01 (0.55)	−0.30 (0.31)	−1.24*** (0.28)	0.04 (0.34)
Services	−0.14 (0.28)	−1.72** (0.71)	0.61* (0.33)	−2.44*** (0.60)	0.67* (0.33)
Services^2	0.0004 (0.003)	0.03** (0.01)	−0.01* (0.003)	0.01** (0.004)	−0.01** (0.
Data set?	ETD	ETD	ETD	ETD	GGDC+Mensah et al. (2018
Controls?	Yes	Yes	Yes	Yes	Yes
Period Dummies?	Yes	Yes	Yes	Yes	Yes
Number of obs	258	81	102	75	366
F statistic	3.61***	7.30***	17.06***	3.60**	3.35***

Note: *. ** and *** denote significance at 10. 5 and 1 per cent level respectively; standard errors in parenthesis. Manufacturing, Nonmanufacturing, and Services are employment shares. Controls are Per capita income, trade (as ratio of GDP), government consumption (as ratio of GDP), and human capital (years of schooling).

Source: Our estimates, based on ETD and data from *World Development Indicators*.

between services employment share and inequality – the coefficient on services employment share is negative and significant, and that for the square of the services employment share, it is positive and significant (Col. I). For structurally developing countries, we observe an opposite relationship between services employment share and inequality – increases in services employment share first increase inequality, then decrease it (the coefficient on manufacturing employment share remains statistically insignificant) (Col. (III)). For structurally developed countries, we now observe a discernible effect of manufacturing employment share on inequality, with coefficients on manufacturing employment share and its square terms negative and positive respectively, and both statistically significant (Col. (IV)). Thus, we see a U-shaped relationship between manufacturing employment share and inequality. We also observe a similar U-shaped relationship between services employment share and inequality.

To sum up, the econometrics estimate suggests that there is no overall relationship between manufacturing- and services-driven structural employment on one hand and inequality on the other. However, we do find that there is considerable heterogeneity in the relationship between structural transformation and inequality. For structurally underdeveloped and developed countries, there is a U-shaped relationship between services employment share and inequality, while for structurally developing countries, there is an inverse U-shaped relationship. When it comes to manufacturing employment share, while we do not see any discernible relationship with inequality for structurally underdeveloped or developing countries, we do see a U-shaped relationship for structurally developed countries. Overall, we do not find empirical support for the Kuznets postulate that inequality will increase with structural transformation, and then decrease, either for the entire sample of countries or by stage of structural transformation.

Our findings differ from Baymul and Sen (2020), who find that manufacturing-driven structural transformation decreases inequality, whether using the entire sample or by stage of structural transformation. Baymul and Sen also find that services-driven structural transformation increased inequality for structurally developing countries and decreases it for structurally developed countries. To compare the Baymul–Sen finding with our results, we estimate Equation (6.1) using the data sets that Baymul–Sen use, which are GGDC supplemented by Mensah et al. (2018) (please see Baymul and Sen (2020) for more details). When we do so, we obtain the same finding as Baymul–Sen: increases in manufacturing employment share are associated with a decrease in inequality initially, then an increase (Col. (V)). In contrast, an increase in services employment share is associated with an increase in inequality, then a decrease – the standard inverse U-shaped curve. This suggests that the finding of a negative relationship between manufacturing-driven structural transformation and inequality, and a positive relationship between manufacturing-driven structural transformation and inequality, is conditional on the time-period of the analysis, which is 1960–2012 in Baymul–Sen (GGDC also has several additional countries than ETD, but, as we have noted earlier, the addition of these countries does not lead to a change in the results we obtain in Table 16). Therefore, a key reason for difference in the results is that the data set used by Baymul–Sen has a much longer time series duration than ETD. Clearly, one important implication of the comparison of our results with Baymul–Sen is that the finding of a negative relationship between manufacturing-driven structural transformation and inequality in Baymul–Sen is predicated on within-country variation in structural transformation and inequality, rather than on between-country variation.

6.5 Concluding Remarks

A key policy concern with structural transformation is that while it is associated with rapid economic growth, it can also contribute to growing inequality, as had been suggested by Kuznets. In this section, we examine whether structural transformation leads to higher inequality. We differentiate between manufacturing-driven structural transformation and services-driven structural transformation to take into account the various paths that countries have followed with respect to the movement out of agriculture to manufacturing and services. In contrast to the Kuznets hypothesis, we do not find evidence that the movement of workers to manufacturing or services increases inequality for the entire sample of countries. However, we also find that the relationship between structural transformation and inequality is different for a country at various stages of structural transformation and is different for services as compared to manufacturing. For example, we find a U-shaped relationship between services employment share and inequality for structurally underdeveloped and developed countries but the exact opposite for structurally developing countries. This suggests that there is no unique relationship between structural transformation and inequality at all stages of structural transformation, and it is important from a policy point of view to keep this heterogeneity in mind.

7 So What Have We Learned?

This section summarizes the key findings of the Element and discusses future research directions and some policy options that follow from the analysis presented in the Element. Our approach in this Element was to follow the comparative approach to economic development pioneered by Simon Kuznets, Hollis Chenery, and Moses Syrquin, and revisit the stylized facts of structural transformation, using a high-quality data set of sectoral employment and value added – the Economic Transformation Database. The main advantage of this data set is that it covers a wide range of low- and middle-income countries for a very recent period, 1990–2018. Common to the comparative approach, we searched for 'the existence of common, transnational factors' (Kuznets 1959) using a typology of stages of structural transformation where we classified countries in Section 2 as structurally underdeveloped, structurally developing, and structurally developed, depending on the proportion of workers in agriculture, manufacturing, and services at the end of our period of analysis.

One of the striking findings of the earlier comparative approach to economic development was the universal inverse association of income and the share of agriculture in income and employment. In Section 3, we find that this inverse association between the share of workers in agriculture and income also holds with more recent data. However, the conventional path of structural transformation as seen by the earlier comparative approach, where workers move first from agriculture to manufacturing, and then on to services, does not find clear support in our analysis of the patterns of structural transformation. Instead, we document a different path of structural transformation for structurally underdeveloped countries, where workers are moving directly from agriculture to non-business services, which as a sector does not have the same productivity gains that we observe in manufacturing (though we also observe an increase in manufacturing employment share as well for the more recent period). This suggests the path of structural transformation that has been witnessed by the high-income countries as well as many countries in East Asia may not be the only route to economic development in contemporary settings What we are observing are 'varieties of structural transformation', rather than a single unified path of structural transformation. This is important to keep in mind when we assess policy options, especially for low-income countries.

As we discussed in Section 4, the theoretical approaches to structural transformation broadly focus on two classes of explanations: (a) unbalanced productivity growth, where increases in agricultural productivity imply that countries only need a smaller number of workers in agriculture to feed the population, and (b) income effects: as countries become richer, households spend a lower proportion of their incomes on food, so that workers relocate to manufacturing and services sectors. In our analysis of the drivers of structural transformation in Section 5, we find empirical support for both explanations. This is not surprising, as the earlier comparative approach had already noted that 'neither structural change nor growth in GDP is an exogenous variable; both result from a complex of interacting causes on the supply side and the demand side' (Matthews et al. 1982: 250). We also find that standard mainstream models of structural transformation (as the one proposed by Duarte and Restuccia 2010) do not adequately explain patterns of structural transformation, especially in the low-income world. We also examine the role of globalization in structural transformation, and find that whether globalization affects structural transformation depends on whether we are looking at manufacturing- versus services-driven structural transformation, whether globalization is measured using trade openness or foreign direct investment inflows, and which stage of structural transformation a particular country is in. This suggests a more nuanced picture of globalization's effects than is conventionally portrayed in the literature.

Finally, in Section 6, we do not find evidence of the Kuznets process – that is, neither manufacturing- nor services-driven structural transformation unambiguously increases inequality for the entire sample of fifty-one countries. Instead, we find that the relationship between structural transformation and inequality depends on the stage of structural transformation, and whether we are looking at manufacturing- or services-driven structural transformation. Here, again, we find the evidence on the Kuznets process is more nuanced than has been generally found in the previous literature.

Further Research Directions

While there has been a vast amount of research, both theoretically and empirically oriented, that has taken place on understanding the patterns of structural transformation in recent years, three important research gaps remain. Perhaps the most important research gap is that much of the literature on developing countries has focused on middle-income countries and the now-rich countries of East Asia, while we know relatively little about what explains the different routes to structural transformation that low-income countries are taking. This is in part related to the lack of reliable data on structural transformation, and with the release of Economic Transformation Database, researchers now have access to a relatively long time-series data for many low-income countries in Africa and Asia.

A second research gap is to do with our limited knowledge of the role of technology in shaping patterns of structural transformation going forward. With routine biased technological change increasingly leading to polarization of employment and earnings in developed and developing countries (see Autor et al. (2003) for evidence on developed countries and Gradin et al. (2023) for evidence on developing countries), an emerging literature has been looking at new models of structural change focusing on workers' tasks instead of sectors (see Duerneker and Herrendorf 2022). This literature highlights the increasing relevance of tasks and occupations as units of analysis for studying structural change instead of sectors as has been the case in the conventional approach to structural transformation.

A third research gap is to do with the role of sectoral productivity gaps in accounting for differences in income per capita across countries (Hsieh and Klenow 2007; Herrendorf and Valentinyi 2012; Gollin et al. 2014). An initial set of studies find that specific sectors matter in explaining differences in per capita income differences across countries. Duarte and Restuccia (2020) show that eliminating cross-country differences in non-traditional services lowers aggregate income disparity by 58 per cent, which is equivalent to an eightfold reduction in cross-country income gaps. More research is needed in understanding the role of other key sectors and what may eliminate sectoral productivity gaps across countries (see Paul and Sen (2022) for an initial exploration on the role of productivity gaps in investment goods).

Policy Options

What would our findings suggest for a policymaker in a low- or middle-income country, where the majority of workers remain in agriculture, and where the movement of workers to manufacturing or services has been slow? Our advice to policymakers would depend on which stage of structural transformation a country is in. If the country is structurally underdeveloped, where the priority for a policymaker would be to move workers as quickly, as possibly from agriculture, manufacturing would still remain the best option for the possibility of structural transformation, when the move to business services does not seem likely till the country has reached a certain level of economic development (as we observed in Section 4). However, as we have also observed in Section 4, manufacturing productivity is quite low in these countries, as compared to structurally developing and developed countries.[40] So the priority should also be to increase the productivity of the manufacturing sector so that when workers move to this sector from agriculture, they have the possibility of earning significantly higher income than in agriculture. This would only be possible if manufacturing is a high-productivity sector. The challenge here is that for many low-income countries, especially in sub-Saharan Africa, jobs are being generated in the low-productivity informal manufacturing sector while the more productive firms are in the low-employment-generating formal manufacturing sector (Diao et al. 2021. This implies *a two-pronged strategy*, where policies to increase productivity in the informal manufacturing sector are combined with policies to increase employment intensity in the formal manufacturing sector. What would these policies look like? For the informal manufacturing sector,

---

[40] This is also observed by McMillan and Zeufack (2022), who find that in several African countries, the manufacturing sector is not contributing to economy-wide productivity growth. Kruse et al. (2021) also find that most of the employment growth in sub-Saharan Africa in the manufacturing sector has been in the informal sector in recent decades.

a range of policies could be considered to improve productivity in that sector, such as skills training for enterprise managers and owners, as well as for informal wage labour, and targeted credit policies which allow informal enterprises to grow and reap economies of scale (see Fields 2019; Gang et al. 2022). For increasing the labour intensity of the formal manufacturing sector, policies that incentivise the use of labour by formal firms such as a higher-skilled workforce and relaxation of labour regulations that discourage firms from employing more labour should be considered (see Sen 2008).

For the structurally developing countries, while manufacturing would still remain important for generating jobs and value-added, the priority should be to increase the share of employment and output in the highly productive business services sector. As we have already noted in Section 1, there is a very real possibility for developing countries to increase their integration with the world economy through tradable service sector jobs, in light of the globotics revolution. The priority for policymakers in structurally developing countries is to implement policies that can enhance the global competitiveness of *both* the manufacturing and business services sectors in their economies. As noted by Baldwin and Forslid (2019), policymakers could take the following steps for increasing the competitiveness of the tradable business services sector: 'collecting better data locally, monitoring international developments closely, providing training for local policymakers on digital economy matters, promoting the provision of digital "soft" commerce skills (such as digital marketing and relationship management) as well as hard skills (such as coding), and embracing a "test-and-learn approach" to deal with the uncertainties and rapid pace of change' (Baldwin and Forslid 2019: 33).

For structurally developed countries who are in middle-income status, who are in a favourable position in that most of their workers are out of the agricultural sector, the immediate priority for policymakers would be to enact the deep structural and institutional reforms that are necessary to move their countries to high-income status (in other words, avoid the 'middle income trap', see Gill and Kharas (2007)). This is not as straightforward as it may seem as the real constraints in moving a country from middle-income to high-income status are not economic in nature but political (see Sen and Tyce 2019).

If there is one key takeaway from this Element, it is that we need to recognize that low-income (and some middle-income) countries are now following different paths of structural transformation than that had been experienced by today's high-income countries. The 'varieties of structural transformation' that we observe in contemporary times in developing countries both need a re-evaluation of the conventional view on the process of structural transformation, as well as more creative thinking on the policy options that are possible for low- and middle-income countries, as they strive to catch up with high-income countries.

References

Acemoglu, D. and V. Guerrieri (2008). 'Capital deepening and non-balanced growth'. *Journal of Political Economy*, 116(3): 467–98.

Ackland, R., S. Dowrick and B. Freyens (2013). 'Measuring global poverty: Why PPP Matters'. *Review of Economics and Statistics*, 95: 813–24.

Alcorta, L., N. Foster-McGregor, B. Verspagen and A. Szirmai (eds.) (2021). *New Perspectives on Structural Change: Causes and Consequences of Structural Change in the Global Economy*. Oxford: Oxford University Press.

Alisjahbana, A., K. Sen, A. Sumner and A. Yusuf (2022). *The Developer's Dilemma, Structural Transformation, Inequality Dynamics and Inclusive Growth*. Oxford: Oxford University Press.

Amirapu, A., and A. Subramanian (2015). Manufacturing or Services? The Indian Illustration of a Development Dilemma. Centre for Global Development Working Paper No. 409. Washington D.C.: Centre for Global Development.

Anand, S. and S. R. Kanbur (1993a). 'The Kuznets process and the inequality: Development relationship'. *Journal of Development Economics*, 40(1): 25–52.

Anand, S. and S. R. Kanbur (1993b). 'Inequality and development a critique'. *Journal of Development Economics*, 41(1): 19–43.

Anzolin, G., A. Andreoni, and A. Zanfei (2022). 'What is driving robotisation in the automotive vale chain? Empirical evidence on the role of FDI and domestic capabilities in technology adoption'. *Technovation*, 115. https://doi.org/10.1016/j.technovation.2022.102476.

Arndt, C., A. McKay, and F. Tarp (2016). *Growth and Poverty in Sub-Saharan Africa*. Oxford: Oxford University Press.

Athukorala, P. and K. Sen (2014). 'Industrialization, employment and poverty'. In P. Athukorala, J. Weiss, and M. Tribe, eds., *Routledge Handbook of Industry and Development*. London: Routledge, pp. 84–96.

Autor, D. H., F. Levy, and R. Murnane (2003). 'The skill content of recent technological change: An empirical exploration'. *Quarterly Journal of Economics*, 118(4): 1279–333.

Balassa, B. (1982). *Development Strategies in Semi-Industrial Economies*. Baltimore: Johns Hopkins University Press.

Baldwin, R. and R. Forslid (2019). Globotics and Development: When Manufacturing are Jobless and Services are Tradable. UNU-WIDER Working Paper No. 94/2019. Helsinki: UNU-WIDER.

Basu, K. (1989). *Analytical Development Economics*. Cambridge, MA: MIT Press.

Baumol, W. (1967). 'Macroeconomics of unbalanced growth: The anatomy of urban crisis'. *American Economic Review*, 57(3): 415–26.

Baymul, C. and K. Sen (2019). 'Kuznets revisited: What do we know about the relationship between structural transformation and inequality?' *Asian Development Review*, 36(1): 136–67.

Baymul, C. and K. Sen (2020). 'Was Kuznets right? New evidence on the relationship between structural transformation and inequality'. *Journal of Development Studies*, 56(9): 1643–62.

Bhagwati, J. N. (1988). 'Export promoting trade strategy: Issues and evidence'. *World Bank Research Observer*, 3: 27–52.

Blomström, M. and A. Kokko (2002). FDI and Human Capital: A Research Agenda, OECD Development Centre Working Paper No. 195. Paris: OECD.

Brooks, D. and H. Hill (2004). *Managing FDI in a Globalizing Economy: Asian Experiences*. Manila: Asian Development Bank.

Buera, F. J. and J. P. Kaboski (2009). 'Can traditional theories of structural change fit the data?'. *Journal of European Economic Association*, 7(2–3): 469–77.

Castello-Climent, A. and R. Doménech (2014). Human Capital and Income Inequality: Some Facts and Some Puzzles. BBVA Research Working Paper No. 12/ 28. Madrid: BBVA.

Chenery, H. B. (1982). Industrialization and Growth: The Experience of Large Countries, World Bank Staff Working Paper No. 539. Washington, DC: The World Bank.

Chenery, H. B. (1988). 'Introduction to part 2'. In H. B. Chenery and T. N. Srinivasan, eds., *Handbook of Development Economics* (vol. 1). Amsterdam: North-Holland.

Chenery, H. B. and M. Syrquin (1975). *Patterns of Development, 1950–1970*. Delhi: Oxford University Press.

Chenery, H. B. and L. Taylor (1968). 'Development patterns: Among countries and over time'. *The Review of Economics and Statistics*, 50: 391–416.

Clark, C. (1940). *The Conditions of Economic Progress*. London: Macmillan.

Comin, D., D. Lashkari, and M. Mestieri (2021). 'Structural change with long-run income and price effects'. *Econometrica*, 89(1): 311–74.

Dabla-Norris, E., A. Thomas, R. Al Garcia-Verdu, and Y. Chen (2013). Benchmarking Structural Transformation across the World. IMF Working Paper. WP/13/176, Washington D.C.: International Monetary Fund.

Dabla-Norris, M. E., M. K. Kochhar, M. N. Suphaphiphat, M. F. Ricka, and E. Tsounta (2015). *Causes and Consequences of Income Inequality: A Global Perspective*. Washington, DC: International Monetary Fund.

De Vries, G., L. Arfelt, D. Drees, et al. (2021). *The Economic Transformation Database (ETD): Content, Sources, and Methods*. WIDER Technical Note 2/ 2021. Helsinki: UNU-WIDER.

Diao, X., M. Ellis, M. McMillan, and D. Rodrik (2021). Africa's Manufacturing Puzzle: Evidence from Tanzanian and Ethiopian Firms. Working Paper No. 28344. Washington, DC: National Bureau of Economic Research.

Diao, X., M. McMillan, and D. Rodrik (2017). The Recent Growth Boom in Developing Economies: A Structural Change Perspective. Working Paper No. 23132. Washington, DC: National Bureau of Economic Research.

Duarte, M. and D. Restuccia (2010). 'The role of structural transformation in aggregate productivity'. *The Quarterly Journal of Economics*, 125(1): 129–73.

Duarte, M. and D. Restuccia (2020). 'Relative prices and sectoral productivity'. *Journal of the European Economic Association*, 18(3): 1400–43.

Duernecker, G. and B. Herredorf (2022). 'Structural transformation of occupation employment'. *Economica*.

Dunning, J. (1993). *Multinational Enterprises and the Global Economy*. New York: Addison Wesley.

Feenstra, R. and G. Hanson (2003). 'Global production sharing and rising inequality: A survey of trade and wage'. In E. K. Choi and J. Harrigan, eds., *Handbook of International Trade*. Malden, MA: Blackwell. 146–185.

Feenstra, R. C., R. Inklaar, and M. P. Timmer (2015). 'The next generation of the Penn World Table'. *American Economic Review*, 105(10): 3150–82.

Felipe, J. and A. Mehta (2016). 'Deindustrialization? A global perspective'. *Economics Letters*, 149(C): 148–51.

Felipe, J., A. Mehta, and C. Rhee (2015). Manufacturing Matters . . . but it's the Jobs that Count. Asian Development Bank Economics and Research Department Working Paper No. 420. Manila: Asian Development Bank.

Fields, G. (2004). 'Dualism in the labour market: A perspective on the Lewis Model after half a century'. *The Manchester School*, 72(6): 724–35.

Fields, G. (2019). 'Self-employment and poverty in developing countries'. *IZA World of Labour*, 60(2): 1–10.

Fujiwara, I. and K. Matsuyama (2020). A Technology Gap Model of Premature Deindustrialization, Working Paper No. 15530. London: Centre for Economic Policy Research.

Gaddis, I., G. Oseni, A. Palacios-Lopez, and J. Pieters (2020). Who Is Employed? Evidence from SubSaharan Africa on Redefining Employment. World Bank Policy Research Working Paper No. 9370. Washington, DC: The World Bank.

Galbraith, J. K., B. Halbach, A. Malinowska, A. Shams, and W. Zhang (2014). UTIP Global Inequality Data Sets, 1963–2008: Updates, Revisions and Data Checks, UTIP Working Paper No. 68. Austin: University of Texas.

Gang, I., R. Rajesh, and K. Sen (2022). 'Finance, gender, and entrepreneurship: India's informal sector firms'. *Journal of Development Studies*. 58(7): 1382–1402.

Gill, I. and H. Kharas (2007). *An East Asian Renaissance: Ideas for Economic Growth*. Washington, DC: World Bank.

Goldberg, P. K. and N. Pavcnik (2007). 'Distributional effects of globalization in developing countries'. *Journal of Economic Perspectives*, 45(1): 39–82.

Gollin, D. (2014). 'The Lewis model: A sixty year retrospective'. *Journal of Economic Perspectives*, 28(3): 71–88.

Gollin, D. (2018). Structural Transformation and Growth without Industrialisation, Pathways to Prosperity Commission Background Paper Series No. 2. Oxford: United Kingdom. Oxford University.

Gollin, D., D. Lagakos, and M. Waugh (2014). 'The agricultural productivity gap in developing countries'. *Quarterly Journal of Economics*, 129(2): 939–93.

Gradin, C. (2021), "WIID Companion: Integrated and Standardized Series", WIDER Technical Note 8/2021, Helsinki: UNU-WIDER.

Gradin, C., P. Lewandowski, S. Schotte, and K. Sen (2023). *Tasks, Skills and Institutions: The Changing Nature of Work and Inequality*. Oxford: Oxford University Press.

Haraguchi, N., C. F. C. Cheng, and E. Smeets (2017). 'The importance of manufacturing in economic development: Has this changed?'. *World Development*, 93(C): 293–315.

Hayami, Y. and V. Ruttan (1985). *Agricultural Development: An International Perspective*. Baltimore: John Hopkins University Press.

Herrendorf, B., R. Rogerson, and A. Valentinyi (2014). 'Growth and structural transformation'. *Handbook of Economic Growth*, 2: 855–941.

Herrendorf, B. and A. Valentinyi (2012). 'Which sectors make poor countries so unproductive?' *Journal of the European Economic Association*, 10(2): 323–41.

Hsieh, C.-T. and P. Klenow (2007). 'Relative prices and relative prosperity'. *American Economic Review*, 97: 562–85.

Huneeus, F. and R. Rogerson (2020). Heterogenous Paths of Industrialization, Working Paper No. 27580. Washington, DC: National Bureau of Economic Research.

International Comparison Program (2017). Washington, DC: The World Bank.

International Monetary Fund (IMF) (2018). *World Economic Outlook: Cyclical Upswing, Structural Change*. Washington, DC: International Monetary Fund.

Jaumotte, F., S. Lall, and C. Papageorgiou (2013). 'Rising income inequality: Technology, or trade and financial globalization?' *IMF Economic Review*, 61(2): 271–309.

Kanbur, R. (2017). Structural Transformation and Income Distribution: Kuznets and Beyond. Charles H. Dyson School of Applied Economics and Management, Cornell University, Working Paper No. 01.Cornell University.

Klasen, S. (2019). 'What explains uneven female labour force participation levels and trends in developing countries?' *The World Bank Research Observer*, 34(2): 161–97. Ithaca.

Kongsamut, P., S. Rebelo, and D. Xie (2001). 'Beyond balanced growth' *Review of Economic Studies*, 68(4): 869–82.

Krueger, A. O. (1977). 'Growth, distortions and patterns of trade among many countries'. *Princeton Studies in International Finance*, 40: 1–50.

Krueger, A. O. (1978). 'Alternate trade strategies and employment in LDCs'. *American Economic Review*, 68(2): 270–74.

Krueger, A. O. (1980). *Trade and Employment in Developing Countries: Synthesis and Conclusion*. Chicago: University of Chicago Press.

Kruse, H., E. Mensah, K. Sen, and G. de Vries (2021). A Manufacturing Renaissance? Industrialization Trends in the Developing World. WIDER Working Paper No. 28/2021. Helsinki: UNU-WIDER.

Kuznets, S. (1955). 'Economic growth and income inequality'. *American Economic Review*, 45(1): 1–28.

Kuznets, S. (1959). 'On the comparative structure of economic structure and the growth of Nations'. In R. Goldsmith, ed., *The Comparative Study of Economic Growth and Structure*. 162–176. Washington, DC: National Bureau of Economics Research.

Kuznets, S. (1965). *Economic Growth and Structure: Selected Essays*. New York: Norton.

Kuznets, S. (1966). *Modern Economic Growth: Rate, Structure, and Spread* (vol. 2). New Haven: Yale University Press.

Kuznets, S. (1973). 'Modern economic growth: Findings and reflections'. *American Economic Review*, 63(3): 247–58.

Kuznets, S. and J. T. Murphy (1966). *Modern Economic Growth: Rate, Structure, and Spread* (vol. 2). New Haven: Yale University Press.

Leamer, E. E. (1987). 'Paths of development in the three-factor n-good general equilibrium model'. *Journal of Political Economy*, 95(5): 961–99.

Lewis, A. (1954). 'Economic development with unlimited supplies of labour'. *The Manchester School*, 22(2): 139–91.

Lewis, L. T., R. Morduch, M. Sposi, and J. Zhang (2022). 'Structural change and global trade'. *Journal of European Economic Association*, 20(1): 476–512.

Matsuyama, K. (2009). 'Structural change in an interdependent world: A global view of manufacturing decline'. *Journal of European Economic Association*, 7(2–3): 478–86.

Matthews, R. C. O., C. Feinstein, and C. Odling-Smee (1982). *British Economic Growth*. Oxford: Oxford University Press.

McMillan, M., D. Rodrik, and Í. Verduzco-Gallo (2014). 'Globalization, structural change, and productivity growth, with an update on Africa'. *World Development*, 63(C): 11–32.

McMillan, M. and A. Zeufack (2022). 'Labour productivity growth and industrialization in Africa'. *Journal of Economic Perspectives*, 36(1): 3–32.

Mensah, E., S. Owusu, N. Foster-McGregor, and A. Szirmai (2018). Structural Change, Productivity Growth and Labour Market Turbulence in Africa. UNU-MERIT Working Paper No. 2018–025. Maastricht: UNU-MERIT.

Nayyar, D. (2019). *Resurgent Asia: Diversity in Development*. Oxford: Oxford University Press.

Nayyar, G., M. Cruz, and L. Zhu (2018). Does Premature Deindustrialization Matter? The Role of Manufacturing and Services in Development, Policy Research Paper No. 8596, Washington, DC: The World Bank.

Nayyar, G., M. Hallward-Driemeier, and E. Davies (2021). *At Your Service?: The Promise of Services-Led Development*. Washington, DC: The World Bank.

Newfarmer, R., J. Page, and F. Tarp (2018). *Industries without Smokestacks: Industrialization in Africa Reconsidered*. Oxford: Oxford University Press.

Ngai, R. and C. Pissarides (2007). 'Structural change in a multisector model of growth'. *American Economic Review*, 97(1): 429–43.

Paul, S. and K. Sen (2022). *Intersectoral Implications of Construction Productivity*. Mimeo. Manchester.

Pahl, S. and M. Timmer (2019). Do global value chains enhance economic upgrading?' *Journal of Development Studies*, 5(9): 1683–705.

Ranis, G. and J. C. H. Fei (1961). 'A theory of economic development'. *American Economic Review*, 51(4): 533–65.

Riedel, J. (1988). 'Economic development in East Asia: Doing what comes naturally?' In H. Hughes, ed., *Achieving Industrialisation in East Asia*. 1–38. Cambridge: Cambridge University Press.

Robinson, S. (1976). 'A note on the U hypothesis relating income inequality and economic development'. *American Economic Review*, 66: 437–40.

Rodrik, D. (1998). 'Why do more open economies have bigger governments?' *Journal of Political Economy*, 106(5): 997–1032.

Rodrik, D. (2016). 'Premature deindustrialization'. *Journal of Economic Growth*, 21(1): 1–33.

Rodrik, D. (2018). New Technologies, Global Value Chains and Developing Economies. Background Paper No. 1. Oxford: Pathways for Prosperity Commission.

Rogerson, R. (2007). Structural Transformation and the Deterioration of European Labour Market Outcomes. NBER Working Paper Series No. 12889. Washington D.C.: NBER.

Roope, L., M. Nino-Zarazua, and F. Tarp (2018). 'How polarized is the global income distribution?', *Economic Letters*, 167: 86–89.

Rostow, W. W. (1960). *The Stages of Economic Growth*. London: W. W. Norton.

Sen, K. (2008). *Trade Policy, Inequality and Performance in Indian Manufacturing*. London: Routledge.

Sen, K. (2019a). 'What explains the job creating potential of industrialisation in the developing world?' *Journal of Development Studies*, 55(4): 1565–83.

Sen, K. (2019b). 'Structural transformation around the world: Patterns and drivers'. *Asian Development Review*, 36(2): 1–31.

Sen, K. and M. Tyce (2019). 'The elusive quest for high income status: Malaysia and Thailand in the post-crisis years'. *Structural Change and Economic Dynamics*, 48(1): 117–35.

Sposi, M. (2019). 'Evolving comparative advantage, sectoral linkages, and structural change'. *Journal of Monetary Economics*, 103(C): 75–87.

Sposi, M., K.-M. Yi, and J. Zhang (2021). *Deindustrialization and Industry Polarization*. STEG Working Paper Series, WP011, London: CEPR.

Syrquin, M. (1988). 'Patterns of structural change'. In H. Chenery and T. N. Srinivasan, eds., *Handbook of Development Economics* (vol. 1). 203–273. Amsterdam: North-Holland.

Syrquin, M. and H. Chenery (1989). 'Three decades of industrialization'. *World Bank Economic Review*, 3(2): 145–81.

Timmer, C. P. (2013). Managing Structural Transformation: A Political Economy Perspective, WIDER Annual Lecture No. 18. Helsinki: UNU-WIDER.

Timmer, M. P. and G. J. de Vries (2009). 'Structural change and growth accelerations in Asia and Latin America: A new sectoral data set'. *Cliometrica*, 3(2): 165–90.

Timmer, M. P., G. J. de Vries, and K. de Vries (2015). 'Patterns of structural change in developing countries'. In J. Weiss and M. Tribe, eds., *Routledge Handbook of Industry and Development*. London: Routledge, pp. 65–83.

Tregenna, F. (2014). 'A new theoretical analysis of deindustrialisation'. *Cambridge Journal of Economics*, 38(6): 1373–90.

United Nations (2009). *System of National Accounts 2008*. Geneva: United Nations.

United Nations Industrial Development Organisation (UNIDO) (2013). *Sustaining Employment Growth: The Role of Manufacturing and Structural Change*. Industrial Development Report 2013. Geneva: UNIDO.

United Nations Industrial Development Organisation (UNIDO) (2022). *The Future of Industrialization in a Post-Pandemic World*. Industrial Development Report 2022. Geneva: UNIDO.

Valentinyi, A. (2021). Structural Transformation, Input-Output Networks, and Productivity Growth, Structural Transformation and Economic Growth (STEG) Pathfinding Paper. London: CEPR, 1–35.

Wood, A. (1994). *North-South Trade, Employment and Inequality: Changing Fortunes in a Skill-Driven World*. Oxford: Clarendon Press.

Wood, A. (2003). *Could Africa be like America? Annual Bank Conference on Development Economics*. Washington, DC: World Bank.

Wood, A. (2017). Variation in Structural Change around the World, 1985–2015. WIDER Working Paper No. 2017/34. Helsinki: UNU-WIDER.

World Bank (2017). *Trouble in the Making? The Future of Manufacturing-Led Development*. Washington, DC: The World Bank.

World Bank (2020). *Trading for Development in the Age of Global Value Chains*. Washington, DC: World Bank.

Cambridge Elements ≡

Development Economics

Series Editor-in-Chief
Kunal Sen
UNU-WIDER and University of Manchester

Kunal Sen, UNU-WIDER Director, is Editor-in-Chief of the Cambridge Elements in Development Economics series. Professor Sen has over three decades of experience in academic and applied development economics research, and has carried out extensive work on international finance, the political economy of inclusive growth, the dynamics of poverty, social exclusion, female labour force participation, and the informal sector in developing economies. His research has focused on India, East Asia, and sub-Saharan Africa.

In addition to his work as Professor of Development Economics at the University of Manchester, Kunal has been the Joint Research Director of the Effective States and Inclusive Development (ESID) Research Centre, and a Research Fellow at the Institute for Labor Economics (IZA). He has also served in advisory roles with national governments and bilateral and multilateral development agencies, including the UK's Department for International Development, Asian Development Bank, and the International Development Research Centre.

Thematic Editors
Tony Addison
University of Copenhagen and UNU-WIDER

Tony Addison is a Professor of Economics in the University of Copenhagen's Development Economics Research Group. He is also a Non-Resident Senior Research Fellow at UNU-WIDER, Helsinki, where he was previously the Chief Economist-Deputy Director. In addition, he is Professor of Development Studies at the University of Manchester. His research interests focus on the extractive industries, energy transition, and macroeconomic policy for development.

Chris Barret
Johnson College of Business, Cornell University

Chris Barrett is an agricultural and development economist at Cornell University. He is the Stephen B. and Janice G. Ashley Professor of Applied Economics and Management; and International Professor of Agriculture at the Charles H. Dyson School of Applied Economics and Management. He is also an elected Fellow of the American Association for the Advancement of Science, the Agricultural and Applied Economics Association, and the African Association of Agricultural Economists.

Carlos Gradín
UNU-WIDER and University of Vigo

Carlos Gradín is a UNU-WIDER Research Fellow, and a professor of applied economics at the University of Vigo (on leave). His main research interest is the study of inequalities, with special attention to those that exist between population groups (e.g., by race or sex). His publications have contributed to improving the empirical evidence in developing and developed countries, as well as globally, and to improving the available data and methods used.

Rachel M. Gisselquist
UNU-WIDER

Rachel M. Gisselquist is a Senior Research Fellow and member of the Senior Management Team of UNU-WIDER. She specializes in the comparative politics of developing countries, with particular attention to issues of inequality, ethnic and identity politics, foreign aid and state building, democracy and governance, and sub-Saharan African politics. Dr Gisselquist has edited a dozen collections in these areas, and her articles are published in a range of leading journals.

Shareen Joshi
Georgetown University

Shareen Joshi is an Associate Professor of International Development at Georgetown University's School of Foreign Service in the United States. Her research focuses on issues of inequality, human capital investment and grassroots collective action in South Asia. Her work has been published in the fields of development economics, population studies, environmental studies and gender studies.

Patricia Justino
UNU-WIDER and IDS – UK

Patricia Justino is a Senior Research Fellow at UNU-WIDER and Professorial Fellow at the Institute of Development Studies (IDS) (on leave). Her research focuses on the relationship between political violence, governance and development outcomes. She has published widely in the fields of development economics and political economy and is the co-founder and co-director of the Households in Conflict Network (HiCN).

Marinella Leone
University of Pavia

Marinella Leone is an assistant professor at the Department of Economics and Management, University of Pavia, Italy. She is an applied development economist. Her more recent research focuses on the study of early child development parenting programmes, on education, and gender-based violence. In previous research she investigated the short-, long-term and intergenerational impact of conflicts on health, education and domestic violence. She has published in top journals in economics and development economics.

Jukka Pirttilä
University of Helsinki and UNU-WIDER

Jukka Pirttilä is Professor of Public Economics at the University of Helsinki and VATT Institute for Economic Research. He is also a Non-Resident Senior Research Fellow at UNU-WIDER. His research focuses on tax policy, especially for developing countries. He is a co-principal investigator at the Finnish Centre of Excellence in Tax Systems Research.

Andy Sumner
King's College London and UNU-WIDER

Andy Sumner is Professor of International Development at King's College London; a Non-Resident Senior Fellow at UNU-WIDER and a Fellow of the Academy of Social Sciences. He has published extensively in the areas of poverty, inequality, and economic development.

About the Series

Cambridge Elements in Development Economics is led by UNU-WIDER in partnership with Cambridge University Press. The series publishes authoritative studies on important topics in the field covering both micro and macro aspects of development economics.

United Nations University World Institute for Development Economics Research

United Nations University World Institute for Development Economics Research (UNU-WIDER) provides economic analysis and policy advice aiming to promote sustainable and equitable development for all. The institute began operations in 1985 in Helsinki, Finland, as the first research centre of the United Nations University. Today, it is one of the world's leading development economics think tanks, working closely with a vast network of academic researchers and policy makers, mostly based in the Global South.

Cambridge Elements ☰

Development Economics

Elements in the series

The 1918–20 Influenza Pandemic: A Retrospective in the Time of COVID-19
Prema-chandra Athukorala and Chaturica Athukorala

*Parental Investments and Children's Human Capital in Low-to-Middle-Income
Countries*
Jere R. Behrman

*Great Gatsby and the Global South: Intergenerational Mobility, Income Inequality,
and Development*
Diding Sakri, Andy Sumner and Arief Anshory Yusuf

Varieties of Structural Transformation: Patterns, Determinants, and Consequences
Kunal Sen

A full series listing is available at: www.cambridge.org/CEDE

Printed in the United States
by Baker & Taylor Publisher Services